PRESENTED TO:

Brett Thomas Orton

BY:

Mom & Dad

ON:

June 25, 2002

THE CHILDREN'S DISCOVERY BIBLE

DISCOVERING GOD'S WORD
FOR THE FIRST TIME

*The stories in this book have been placed
in chronological order,
which may not reflect their
order of appearance
in the Bible.*

THE CHILDREN'S DISCOVERY BIBLE

DISCOVERING GOD'S WORD
FOR THE FIRST TIME

Equipping Kids for Life!
Cook Communications Ministries
faithkids.com

Faith Kids® is an imprint of Cook Communications Ministries
Cook Communications, Colorado Springs, CO 80918
Cook Communications, Paris, Ontario
Kingsway Communications, Eastbourne, England

THE CHILDREN'S DISCOVERY BIBLE
© 1996 by Cook Communications Ministries for text and illustrations

Cover design by Granite Design
Creative Director, Brenda Franklin
Contributing Editor, Charlene Hiebert
Executive Editor, Karl Schaller
Illustrations by Drew Rose

First Printing 1996

Printed in the United States of America

05 04 03 02 01 00   5 4 3 2 1

Library of Congress Cataloging-in-Publication Data

The children's discovery Bible /
        p.   cm.
    Summary: A collection of retold stories and memory verses from the Bible.
        ISBN: 0-7814-3499-8
        1. Bible stories, English. [1. Bible stories.] Chariot Books. Title.
BS551.2.C47   1996
220.9'505—dc20

                                        96-28851
                                        CIP
                                        AC

Table of Contents

Old Testament

New Testament

The
OLD
Testament

God Makes Day and Night

Bible story from Genesis 1:1-5,14-18.

In the beginning, God lived, but there was nothing else. No people. No animals. No plants. No sun. No moon. No stars. No world. Nothing.

But God always was. Nobody made Him.

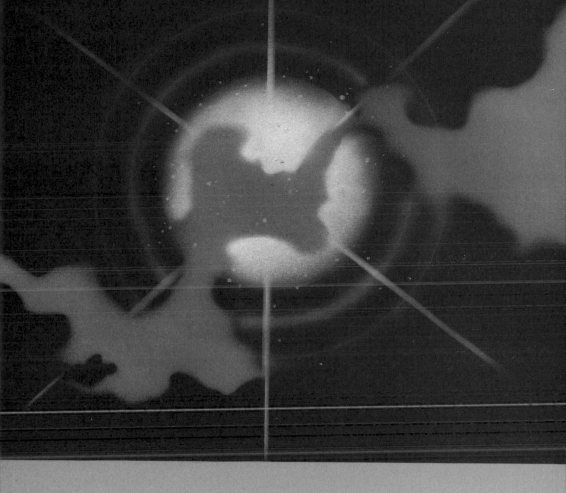

God wanted to make people. But in the beginning He first made some things people would need.

God said, "Let there be light." And there was light. God liked the light He created.

God called the light "day." And He called the darkness "night."

There was evening and there was morning. It was the very first day.

God created lights to shine. He made the sun for the day. He made the moon for the night. He also made stars. He made many, many stars.

He put the lights where they could light the world.

What if it were always dark? Would that be good? No! We could not see and there would be no warm sunlight to help the plants grow.

What if it were always light? Would that be good? No! We need a time to sleep and rest.

God created what we need. He made day and He made night. God is a good creator.

Memory Verse
In the beginning God created the heavens and the earth.

Genesis 1:1

God's Wonderful World

Bible story from Genesis 1:6-13.

God made the whole world. God made the light and gave us day and night. God made the sky above. God made the water below.

God said, "Let the water be in one place, and let there be dry land." It was so. And God liked how it turned out.

But God was not done. God made grass and plants and trees. Everything began to grow. The grass and plants and trees made seeds. The seeds grew. They grew into new grass and plants and trees.

God looked at His world and He liked it!

Memory Verse
For everything God created is good.

I Timothy 4:4a

God Makes Animals

Bible story from Genesis 1:20-25.

God made day and night. He made the sky and water and land. He made the grass and plants and trees.

Then God's world was ready for animals! There was clean air to breathe. There was fresh water to drink and good food to eat.

God said, "Let the water be full of fish. Let birds fly in the sky. Let the land have all kinds of animals that walk and crawl."

God created hundreds and hundreds of different animals. And God liked everything He made!

Memory Verse
The earth is the Lord's, and everything in it.

Psalm 24:1a

God Makes People

Bible story from Genesis 1:26—2:25.

God was ready to make someone very special. He wanted to make someone who could love Him. He wanted to make someone who could take care of the world.

So God made a man. He called the man Adam.

God put Adam in a garden. The garden was very beautiful. Many trees grew there. A river flowed by. Many animals lived there too.

The man ate food from the trees. He took care of the garden. God let him name the animals.

But Adam did not have a helper. There were no other people in the garden.

God said, "The man should not be alone. I will make him a helper." So God created a woman. He named the woman Eve.

The man and the woman could think. They could talk with God. They could be His friends.

God gave them food from the garden. He told them to take care of everything.

The man and woman were happy in the world God made for them.

Finally, God was done with His work. He looked at everything that He made. "I like it all," He said. Then He rested.

Memory Verse
I praise you because I am fearfully and wonderfully made.

Psalm 139:14a

The First Sin

Bible story from Genesis 3.

Adam and Eve were happy. They lived in a beautiful garden. God made the garden for them.

The trees in the garden had fruit. God said, "Enjoy the fruit. It is for you. But one tree is special. Do not eat from it. If you do, I will punish you."

Adam and Eve obeyed God, and they were happy.

But a snake was in the garden. The snake talked to Eve. Actually, Satan talked through the snake.

Eve was near the special tree, and Satan said to Eve, "Did God tell you not to eat this fruit?"

"Yes," Eve said. "We will be punished if we eat it."

"You won't be punished," Satan lied. "You will know good and bad. You will be smart like God."

Eve looked at the tree. The fruit looked so good! She wanted to know everything God knows. So Eve ate some fruit. Then she gave some to Adam. He ate it too.

Later, God came to talk to them. But they hid from Him. They were afraid because they didn't obey.

God said, "You should have obeyed Me. Now I must punish you."

God sent Adam and Eve out of the garden. God said, "You must work hard now. You will not always be happy."

Adam and Eve were sad. They knew they had done wrong. God had to punish them.

Memory Verse
The Lord disciplines those he loves.

Proverbs 3:12a

Cain Gets Into Trouble

Bible story from Genesis 4:1-16.

Because Adam and Eve did not obey God, they had to leave the garden. But they did not forget God, and God still loved them.

Adam and Eve had two boys. One boy's name was Cain. Cain grew up to be a farmer. He planted grain in the field. The other boy was Abel. Abel grew up to be a shepherd. He took care of sheep.

Adam taught the boys to give offerings to God. Abel wanted to please God. So he gave God his best sheep. God was happy with Abel.

Cain gave God some grain from his fields. But Cain didn't care if he pleased God. He did not obey God. So God did not accept Cain's offering. That made Cain very angry!

God said to Cain, "Why are you angry? I will be happy with you if you obey me."

Cain did not listen. He kept doing wrong. One day Cain said to Abel, "Let's go walk to the field." Abel went with Cain. When they were alone, Cain killed his brother Abel.

God said, "Where is your brother?"

"How should I know?" Cain said to God.

"You should know because you killed him," God said. "Now you must go away from home. You will have to move from place to place. The seeds you plant will not grow well anymore."

Cain was sad. And God was sad too. Cain should have stopped doing wrong when God told him to.

Memory Verse
God disciplines us for our good.

Hebrews 12:10b

Noah Obeys God

Bible story from Genesis 6:9—7:24.

Many years went by after God made people. Many families lived in the world. But most of them did not obey God. Only Noah obeyed God.

One day God told Noah, "I must punish the people because they do not obey me. A big flood will cover the land. But I will keep your family safe." God told Noah to build a big boat called an ark.

God told Noah, "Take two animals of every kind into the ark. Go into the ark with your family and I will shut the door." Noah obeyed God.

Soon the rain came. It rained for more than a month! Water covered everything. But Noah and his family were safe. He was glad he had obeyed God.

Memory Verse
Whoever trusts in the Lord is kept safe

Proverbs 29:25b

Noah Thanks God

Bible story from Genesis 8:1—9:17.

Noah and his family were in the ark for a long time. The animals were in the ark too.

The rain finally stopped, but the water still covered the ground. The ark floated on the water. Then it came to the top of a mountain.

Noah opened a window. All he could see was water.

Noah let a dove fly out of the ark. The bird came back with
a leaf in its beak. "Trees are growing again," Noah said.
"That means the water is lower."

Noah waited seven more days. Then he let the dove out
again. This time the dove did not come back. It
had found a dry home.

God said, "You may leave the ark now, and let all
of the animals go." So they did.

"We obeyed God, and God kept us safe," Noah said to his family. Noah built an altar, and they all thanked God for keeping them safe.

God was happy. He liked what Noah did. God said, "I will make you a promise. There will always be spring and fall, summer and winter. And I will never send a great flood to cover the whole earth again."

Then God said, "I will make a rainbow in the sky. When you see the rainbow, remember my promise."

"Thank you, God," said Noah and his family. "Thank you for keeping us safe. Thank you for keeping the animals safe too."

Memory Verse
I can do everything through him who gives me strength.

Philippians 4:13

The Tower of Babel

Bible story from Genesis 11:1-9.

After the big flood, Noah's three sons and their wives had many children. When these children grew up, they had many children too. Soon the world began to fill with people again.

Everyone talked the same language. They said, "Come, let's make bricks and build a city with a big tower. We can build it tall enough to reach heaven."

God saw what the people were doing. He was not happy. "This will lead to nothing good," He said. "I want people to spread out and fill the world."

God made every family talk a different language. No one understood his neighbor. "Stop babbling!" they said to each other. Work soon stopped on the tower, and the people packed up and moved away.

Memory Verse
Those who walk in pride he is able to humble.

Daniel 4:37b

God Calls Abraham

Bible story from Genesis 11:31—12:9.

Abraham lived in a big city. Most of the people in the city did not know God. They worshiped the moon. Abraham knew God and wanted to obey Him.

One day God called Abraham to do something special. God said, "Leave your home, Abraham. I will show you a new land." So Abraham moved.

First he moved to a new city. But God said to him again, "Leave your home. I will show you a new land. I will be with you and help you. I will give you a great family. You will be very special."

So Abraham left. He took his wife, Sarah, with him. He took his nephew, Lot. He took all of his servants. He took his sheep and cows.

The family walked for a long time. It was a hard trip. But God showed them where to go.

One day they came to a new land. God said to Abraham, "This will be your land. I am giving it to you and to your family."

Abraham built an altar. He talked to God there. Then he set up his tent in his new homeland. His family put up their tents too.

God told Abraham, "Obey Me and do what is right. I will be with you and help you. I will give you a great family. You will be very special."

Abraham looked at the new land. It was his land! God had called him to move there.

Memory Verse
Show me your ways, O Lord, teach me your paths.

Psalm 25:4

Abraham and Sarah Wait for God's Answer

Bible story from
Genesis 15:1-5;
17:15-21;21:-1-3.

Year after year Abraham and Sarah prayed that God would give them a child. God promised to do it, but they had to wait. When they had waited a long time, they wondered, "Will God ever answer our prayer?"

One night God said, "Don't worry, Abraham."

God told Abraham to look at the night sky. "Try to count the stars," God said. "That's how many children and grandchildren and great-grandchildren and great-great-grandchildren I will give you!" What a big family Abraham would have some day!

So Abraham and Sarah kept waiting for God to answer their prayer. They grew very old. "We are too old," they said. "God will never give us a baby now." It seemed impossible they would ever have a child.

Then one day God said, "Abraham, I am going to answer your prayer. You and Sarah are going to have a baby. You will name him Isaac."

Abraham and Sarah said, "We have prayed for so long, and we have waited a long, long time. Will God really give us a baby now when we are old?"

God answered their prayers. He gave them a baby boy! Abraham and Sarah named him Isaac which means "he laughs."

That was a good name because baby Isaac made Abraham and Sarah laugh with joy.

How good God was to answer their prayer! And all the time they waited for His answer, God did not forget Abraham and Sarah. His answer finally came at just the right time.

Memory Verse
Wait for the Lord; be strong and take heart and wait for the Lord.
Psalm 27:14

A Wife for Isaac

Bible story from Genesis 24.

Isaac was not little anymore. He was a grown-up man. It was time he had a wife. Abraham wanted Isaac to have a wife who loved God. Abraham asked his best servant to help. "Go to the land where I once lived and find Isaac a good wife. God will help you."

The servant packed some food, water, and gifts onto some camels. The gifts were for Isaac's new wife.

The servant traveled many days on the camel. He came to a city where Abraham once lived. The servant stopped to rest by a well. He prayed to God, "Help me find a wife for Isaac. I'll ask a young girl for water. I'll see if she gives the camels water too. If she does, she will be right for Isaac."

A girl came to the well. She filled her pitcher with water. The servant went over to the girl. "May I have a drink?" he asked.

"Yes," she answered as she handed him some water to drink. "I'll give your camels a drink too."

Abraham's servant smiled. God had made things turn out well. "Tell me your name," the servant asked.

"I am Rebekah," she said. Then she invited the servant to meet her family and spend the night at her home.

The servant told Rebekah's family why he had come and he gave Rebekah the gifts.

Rebekah and her family agreed that she would marry Isaac even though she had never met him.

The next day Rebekah and the servant traveled back to Isaac's home. When Isaac and Rebekah met, they fell in love. God made things turn out well for them.

Memory Verse
Praise the Lord, O my soul, and forget not all his benefits.

Psalm 103:2

Jacob Tricks His Family

Bible story from Genesis 25:27-34; 27:1-45.

Esau and Jacob were twin brothers. Esau was born a few minutes before Jacob. That meant that Esau was the oldest son, and that someday he would be the head of the family.

One day while Esau was hunting, Jacob made some soup. When Esau came home he was very hungry. "Give me some soup right away," he said.

Jacob answered, "I'll give you some soup if you give me your place in the family."

Esau didn't think about how special his place in the family was. So he said, "You may have my place."

Many years went by. Isaac grew very old. Isaac was Jacob and Esau's father. "I will bless you, Esau," said Isaac. "But first bring me some deer meat to eat."

Jacob wanted to be blessed. So while Esau went hunting, Jacob and his mother planned a trick.

Jacob's mother cooked some goat meat just the way Isaac liked it. Then she tied the goat skins around Jacob's arms and neck. "Your father is blind. When he touches you and feels the goat hair, he will think you are Esau because Esau has more hair than you. Hurry! Go to your father before Esau gets home."

So Jacob went to his father's tent. He leaned close to Isaac and said, "I am Esau, and I have brought you the meat you asked for. Won't you bless me now?"

Isaac felt Jacob's arms. He thought it was his hairy son Esau. So Isaac blessed Jacob. Isaac prayed, "May God give you many things. May everyone do what you say. You will be the head of the family."

Esau was very angry when he found out what Jacob had done. Jacob had to leave home for a long time.

Memory Verse
Do not steal, do not give false testimony.

Matthew 19:18a

Jacob's Dream

Bible story from Genesis 28:10-22.

Jacob was running away from home. His brother Esau was very angry and wanted to kill him. It was almost night so Jacob stopped to rest. There was no soft bed for him to sleep on, just the hard ground and a rock for his pillow.

Jacob was too tired to care and soon he fell asleep. He dreamed that he saw a ladder that reached all the way to heaven. Angels were going up and down the ladder. At the top stood the Lord God.

God said, "I am the God of your father and grandfather. I will give you and your children the land you are sleeping on if you will make me your God too. I will promise to take care of you."

When Jacob woke up, he poured oil on the stone he used as a pillow. Then he told God, "If You will take care of me and bring me safely back to my father's house someday, You will be my God wherever I go."

Memory Verse
I am with you and will watch over you wherever you go.

Genesis 28:15a

Jealous Brothers

Bible story from Genesis 37.

Joseph had ten older brothers and they were jealous of Joseph. Their father, Jacob, gave Joseph a new coat. This was a very special coat with long sleeves and many bright colors. Jacob had never given the older boys a coat that nice.

One night Joseph had a dream. He dreamed that he and his brothers each had a bundle of grain.

Joseph's bundle of grain stood up. But his brothers' bundles bowed down to Joseph's.

Joseph had another dream. The sun and moon and stars bowed down to him in that dream.

Joseph told his brothers about the dreams. The angry brothers said, "Do you think that someday you will be our king? We will never bow down to you."

One day the older brothers took their sheep to the hills to find green grass. Many days later Jacob said to Joseph, "Go see how your brothers are doing. Then come and tell me."

Joseph put on his beautiful coat and went to find his brothers. When his angry brothers saw him coming, they decided to get rid of him. They took off his coat and threw him into a deep, dry well.

Soon a group of men came by on camels. They were going to the land of Egypt to sell things.

One brother said, "Let's sell Joseph to these men. They will take him to Egypt and sell him as a slave."

So that is what the brothers did. They tore Joseph's beautiful coat and put goat's blood on it. When they got back home, they told their father, Jacob, "Oh, Dad, we found Joseph's coat. A wild animal must have killed him." This news made Jacob very sad.

Memory Verse
Make every effort to live in peace with all men.

Hebrews 12:14a

Joseph Goes to Prison

Bible story from Genesis 39—40.

The men who bought Joseph took him far away to the land of Egypt. And then they sold him to a rich man named Potiphar.

Potiphar liked Joseph. Every job Joseph was given, he did well. One day Potiphar told Joseph, "Joseph, I know that I can trust you to take care of everything I own, my money, my house, and my fields. You will be my chief servant."

One day Potiphar's wife asked Joseph to do something he knew Potiphar wouldn't like. "No!" Joseph told her. "Your husband trusts me. It would be wrong for me to do something like that."

This made Potiphar's wife very angry. "I'll show you!" she said. Then she started to cry and went to Potiphar and told him a lie about Joseph.

Potiphar believed his wife's lie. So he had Joseph thrown into prison.

Joseph was a good helper in prison. Soon he had an important job. He helped watch the other men. Joseph was kind and listened to the other prisoners.

Two men in prison had dreams that worried them. One of the men was the king's baker. The other man was the king's cupbearer.

God let Joseph know what the dreams meant. Joseph told the cupbearer, "In three days you will be let out of prison and given your job back."

Joseph told the baker, "Your dream means that in three days you will die."

Everything Joseph told the two men came true. "Please tell the king about me," he said to the cupbearer. "I am in prison, but I have done nothing wrong." The cupbearer said that he would talk to the king, but he soon forgot all about Joseph.

Memory Verse
Be strong and take heart, all you who hope in the Lord.

Psalm 31:24

Joseph Helps the King

Bible story from Genesis 41:1-40.

Two years went by and Joseph was still in prison. Then one night the king had two strange dreams. He asked his helpers, "Who can tell me what my dreams mean?" No one could answer the king.

Then the cupbearer remembered Joseph. He said, "I know a man who can help you." So the king sent for Joseph.

Joseph told the king, "Your dreams mean that there will be seven good years to grow food. Then there will be seven bad years. Your dreams are a warning to start saving food for the bad years."

The king made Joseph his helper. "I will give you the job of saving food for the bad years. You are no longer a prisoner or a slave. Next to me, you are the most important man in Egypt."

Memory Verse
"Because he loves me," says the Lord, "I will rescue him."

Psalm 91:14a

Joseph Forgives His Brothers

Bible story from Genesis 42:1—47:12.

Now Joseph was the king's helper. During the seven good years he told the people what food to save. He put the food in big barns. When the seven bad years came, he sold the food to the people.

One day ten men came from another country to buy food. They bowed down to Joseph. The ten men were Joseph's brothers! The ones who sold him.

Joseph knew them, but they didn't know him. "Is your father alive?" Joseph asked them. "Do you have a younger brother?"

"Yes, our father is alive and we have a younger brother named Benjamin," the men said.

"One of you stay here in prison and the rest of you go home and get Benjamin," Joseph said.

So one brother stayed in Egypt and the others went home to get Benjamin.

When the brothers came back with Benjamin, Joseph sold them some food. "Benjamin must stay with me," Joseph said.

"No!" all the brothers cried. "We must take Benjamin home. Our father needs him. Keep one of us instead."

Now Joseph knew that his brothers had changed. They were sorry they had made their father sad by selling Joseph. So Joseph invited his brothers to his home for dinner.

They still didn't know who he was. But when he was alone with them, he said, "I am your brother, Joseph. I forgive you for sending me here." Were his brothers ever surprised!

"God wanted me here so that I could help the king save food for everyone," Joseph said. "Now, bring my father to see me." So his brothers did.

Memory Verse
Glorify the Lord with me; let us exalt his name together.

Psalm 34:3

Miriam Does Her Part

Bible story from Exodus 1:1—2:10.

Miriam and her family were Hebrews. The Hebrews were God's people, and they lived in the land of Egypt. One day the king of Egypt said, "There are too many Hebrew people in my land. All the Hebrew baby boys should be killed."

Miriam had a baby brother. She wanted to do her part to help hide him from the king's men.

Miriam watched her mother make a basket bed for the baby. It was like a little boat. Then she and her mother put the baby into the basket and closed the lid.

"We will hide the baby in the weeds that grow along the river," Miriam's mother said. "That way when he cries, no one will hear him. I want you to hide in the weeds too, so you can keep your brother safe."

Soon Miriam saw some women coming to the river. It was the princess and her helpers. The princess was the king's daughter.

As the princess and her helpers walked by the place where Miriam and the baby were hiding, the baby started to cry. "What's that noise?" the princess asked. "It sounds like a baby."

One of her helpers found the basket and brought it to the princess. When the princess opened the basket, she saw the crying baby and picked him up. "It's a Hebrew baby boy!" she said. "I will adopt him and call him Moses."

Miriam ran to the princess and said, "I know someone who can help you take care of this baby."

"Good," the princess said. "Go get this woman." So Miriam ran to get her mother. Miriam was happy to help find her brother a safe new home.

Memory Verse
Do not forget to do good and to share with others.

Hebrews 13:16a

God Gives Moses a Helper

Bible story from Exodus 3:1—4:20.

When Moses grew up, he did not live with the Hebrew people in Egypt where they were slaves. Moses left Egypt and became a shepherd. One day while Moses was with his sheep, he saw a bush that was on fire. But as he watched the bush, he noticed it was not burning up.

Moses walked closer to the bush to look at it. Then he heard a voice call from the bush, "Moses, Moses!"

Moses knew it was God talking. "I am here," he said.

"Take off your shoes, Moses. This place is special because I am here," God said.

Moses took off his dirty shoes and hid his face from God. He was very afraid.

God said, "I am your God, Moses. I have seen the pain of My people, the Hebrews. Go back to Egypt and tell the king to let My people go free. I have a new land for them to live in."

"How can I make the king let the Hebrew people go?" Moses asked God.

"Don't worry. I will be with you to help," said God.

But Moses was still afraid. He asked, "What shall I tell the Hebrew people?"

God answered, "Tell them that I sent you."

Moses was still afraid to do what God asked. "Send someone else," he said. "I do not talk very well."

God answered, "I made your mouth, Moses. I will help you talk. But I will send your brother, Aaron, with you to do this hard thing."

So Moses went back to Egypt and found his brother, Aaron. He was happy that God had given him a helper. And he was happy that God would be helping them too.

Memory Verse
Carry each other's burdens.

Galatians 6:2a

Moses and Aaron Keep Trying

Bible story from Exodus 5:1—10:29.

Moses and Aaron went to the king of Egypt and said, "Let the Hebrew people go. God has a new land for them."

"I do not know your God," said the king. "Why should I do what He says? I will not let the people go." The king was very angry. He made the Hebrew slaves work even harder than before.

Moses told the Hebrew people "God wants us to go to a new land. We must keep on trying to leave."

Then God said to Moses and Aaron, "Go talk to the king again. I will show the king My power. The king will know that I am God."

So Moses and Aaron kept on trying. They said to the king again, "Let God's people go!"

"No!" said the angry king.

But Moses and Aaron kept on trying. They went to the king many times and said, "Let God's people go." But the king would not listen.

Every time the king said no, God made something bad happen to the Egyptians. Their water turned to blood. Then all the frogs hopped out of the water and filled the Egyptians' streets and houses. Then great clouds of flies and big hopping bugs came. A hailstorm smashed all the food the farmers were growing. And the Egyptians' cattle got sick and died.

God made other bad things happen too. But He always kept the Hebrews safe. After each bad thing, Moses and Aaron told the king, "Let God's people go!" But the king said no.

Moses and Aaron knew they should keep trying. With God helping them, the king would soon give in.

Memory Verse
Trust in the Lord and do good.

Psalm 37:3a

A Time to Leave

Bible story from Exodus 11:1—12:51.

One day God told Moses the Hebrews would soon leave Egypt. God said, "One more bad thing will happen. The oldest son in every Egyptian family will die. Then the king will let My people go."

God gave Moses directions for the Hebrew people to follow. Hebrew fathers were to mark their doors with the blood of a lamb. God promised to pass over the homes with the blood and not kill any Hebrew sons.

God also said the Hebrews should fix a Passover meal of lamb and flatbread. They had to eat in a hurry so they would be ready to leave Egypt.

Everything happened just as God said. The king and his people were very sad because their oldest sons died. The king knew he could not win against God. "God's people can leave now," the king told Moses.

Memory Verse
God is our refuge and strength, an ever-present help in trouble.

Psalm 46:1

God Rescues His People

Bible story from Exodus 13:17—15:21.

When Moses and the Hebrew people left Egypt, they did not know the way to the new land God promised them. But they knew God would lead them. They knew nothing was too hard for God.

God sent a big cloud to lead His people in the daytime. At night the cloud glowed like fire and gave them light to see by.

The people followed the cloud. Soon they came to the Red Sea. They put up tents to rest there.

But then the people heard sounds. It was the Egyptian army! The king had sent his men to make the Hebrews go back to Egypt.

The Hebrew people were afraid when they saw the Egyptians coming. The Red Sea was in front of them, and they had no boats they could use to cross it.

"Do not be afraid," said Moses. "God will keep us safe." He knew nothing was too hard for God.

Then God said to Moses, "Hold up your shepherd's rod."

Moses did what God told him. Then God made the wind blow. It moved the water of the Red Sea. Soon there was a dry path through the sea. The people walked across.

The Egyptian army followed behind. But when the Hebrew people were safe, God made the water come back again. The Egyptians drowned in the sea.

Then the Hebrew people sang to God, "You are a great God. Nothing is too hard for our God."

Memory Verse
For nothing is impossible with God.

Luke 1:37

God Gives Water and Food

Bible story from Exodus 15:22—16:36.

Moses and the Hebrew people walked in the desert for three days. They were very hot and thirsty, and there was no water for them to drink.

Then the people saw a spring of water. They ran to the spring for a drink, but the water tasted very bad. The people became angry with Moses. They said, "This is all your fault. You brought us here. We need good water to drink."

Moses asked God to show him what to do. God told him to throw a tree into the bad water. This sounded strange, but Moses did what God said. Somehow the tree made the water taste better. So then the Hebrew people could drink it.

Soon God's cloud began to move and it was time to walk some more. It led the Hebrews to a nice place with wells of clean water and many shade trees. They stayed there for a few days and rested. Then God's cloud moved again and they followed it.

Soon the people became hungry because they ran out of food. They were angry with Moses again. "We are hungry!" they cried.

So Moses talked to God again. He knew God could help him. God told Moses, "I will send you food."

Soon some birds called quail flew by. The people caught the quail and cooked them for supper.

The next morning the people found strange small crumbs scattered all over the ground.

The crumbs were white and tasted good. "The crumbs are food from God," Moses told the people. The people called the food "manna."

God took care of His people while they were in the desert. He always gave them enough food to eat and water to drink.

Memory Verse
And my God will meet all your needs.

Philippians 4:19a

Moses Gets Help

Bible story from Exodus 18:13-27.

Moses had too much work to do! He was the judge for God's people. When the Hebrews had a problem, they came to Moses to ask him what to do.

There were many people with problems. People came to Moses all day long. He could never take time to stop and rest. Then Moses' father-in-law, Jethro, had a good idea.

Jethro said to Moses, "You need help. Teach some other people to be judges so they can help you. If a problem is too hard for them, then the people can come to you for help."

Moses did what Jethro said. More judges could listen to more people. Working together helped everyone.

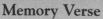

Memory Verse
Now you are the body of Christ, and each one of you is a part of it.
I Corinthians 12:27

God Gives Rules to His People

Bible story from
Exodus 19:1—20:20.

The Hebrew people put up tents and stayed near a big mountain. It was called Mount Sinai.

God spoke to Moses on the top of the mountain and gave him a message for the Hebrew people. "If these people will obey Me," God said, "I will make them My special people. I will always help them."

Moses went down from the mountain. He told the Hebrew people God's words.

"We will obey God," the people told Moses. So Moses went up the mountain again to tell God that the people wanted to obey Him.

God said, "Tell My people to get ready. Soon they will meet Me." The people got ready to meet God just as He told them to do.

Then God came down on the mountain. The people heard His thunder and saw His lightning and they were afraid. They also heard a very loud trumpet and saw a big cloud on the mountaintop.

Then God called Moses up to the mountain again. He gave Moses rules for the people. God said, "I am your God. Love Me. I am the only true God. Worship God, not things. Use God's name the right way. Keep God's day very special. Honor your parents. Do not kill people. Love your own husband and wife.

"Do not steal. Do not tell lies. Do not want what belongs to others."

Then Moses told the people not to be afraid. He said, "God wants you to obey His rules. They will help you love God and others."

Memory Verse
If you love me, you will obey what I command.

John 14:15

Moses Writes Down God's Word

Bible story from Deuteronomy 5:1-7; 6:5-9; 28:1-14; 31:9—32:47.

Moses told the people, "God wants us to obey Him. God wrote ten commandments for us on two stone tablets, so we can know what God wants us to do." Moses read God's words to the people. "Tell your children about God's Word. Talk about His Word everywhere you go."

Then God said to Moses, "Write down a song to help the people remember Me."

Moses wrote down this song: "I will talk about God. He is a great God. He is a good God. Remember what God has done. He came to help us. He took care of us. God will live forever. Be glad, everyone. God will take care of us."

Moses told the people, "This song will help you remember to obey God's Word."

Memory Verse
I have hidden your word in my heart that I might not sin against you.
Psalm 119:11

Trusting God

Bible story from Numbers 13:1—14:35.

The Hebrew people were near Canaan, the new land God had promised to give them. God told Moses to send twelve men to explore the new land. The men came back with lots of fruits and vegetables. "It is a very good land with plenty of crops and fruit," they said.

Ten of the men were afraid, however. They said, "The people of Canaan are big and strong like giants. We cannot win against them if they fight us."

But Joshua and Caleb wanted the people to trust God. "Don't be afraid of those big people. The Lord will be with us," they said. "He will help us take over the new land."

Then God told Moses, "Because Caleb and Joshua trust Me, they will get to live in the new land. But all the other grown-up Hebrew people will not get to live there, because they are afraid. Only their children will go to the new land."

Memory Verse
Whoever trusts in the Lord is kept safe.

Proverbs 29:25b

Crossing the Jordan River

Bible story from
Joshua 1:1-18; 3:1—4:9.

After Moses grew old and died, Joshua became the leader of God's people. One day God said to Joshua, "It is time to lead My people to the new land. Do not be afraid. I will be with you."

Joshua said to the people, "You must get ready. We will cross the Jordan River and go into the new land God has given us."

God also told Joshua, "Have priests carry the ark of the covenant across the river first. Then the people should follow the ark."

The ark was a special box that held a jar of manna and the tablets on which God wrote His ten rules. So Joshua told the people, "We will cross the river now. God will help us. He will stop the water when the priests step into the river."

When the priests carried the ark into the water, the river parted, just like Joshua said it would. God had stopped the water. Now the people had a dry path to walk on.

Memory Verse
For the Lord your God will be with you wherever you go.

Joshua 1:9b

God Wins a Battle

Bible story from Joshua 5:13—6:27.

Joshua and the Hebrew people came into the new land of Canaan. They found out that most of the people living there were their enemies.

The great city of Jericho was near the Jordan River. It had high, stone walls all around it. The king of Jericho was not happy to see the Hebrews coming. "We will fight them if they get too close," he told his soldiers.

Joshua knew that Jericho was an enemy city. God told him, "You will have to fight the people of Jericho, but do not be afraid. I will help you win the battle."

God gave Joshua a special battle plan, and Joshua told the people. They were to march around the walls of Jericho without talking. Four priests would carry the ark while other priests blew horns. The Hebrew people did what God said.

The people marched around the city for six days. Each day they walked around the city one time. Then they went back to their camp. This was just what God had told them to do.

On the seventh day the people marched again. But this time they went around the city seven times.

The last time around, the priests blew their horns. Then all of the people shouted and the city walls fell down.

The people went into the city and took it from their enemies. God showed the people how to win the battle. And they won because they did what He said.

Memory Verse
I will instruct you and teach you in the way you should go.

Psalm 32:8a

Thanking God

Bible story from Leviticus 23:33-44; Nehemiah 8:13-18.

After God helped His people leave Egypt and go to the new land, He wanted the Hebrew people to remember how He helped them. He told them to have a special time every year to remember His help. It was to be a time of thanksgiving.

During this special time the people did not work. They ate a big meal. They stayed in little houses made from tree branches.

The houses helped them remember when they had lived in tents. The people also read from God's Word and thanked Him for His help. They sang songs about how good God is.

God told the people, "This special time will help your children remember how good I have been to the Hebrew people."

Memory Verse
For the Lord is good and his love endures forever.

Psalm 100:5a

King Jabin Causes Trouble

Bible story from Judges 4:1-3.

After many battles, the Hebrew people settled in Canaan, the land God promised to give them. Other people lived in Canaan too. And they did not like sharing the land with the Hebrews.

Jabin was a mighty Canaanite king. He had many soldiers with iron swords, spears, and shields. He also had nine hundred iron chariots. Jabin did not like the Hebrews.

The Hebrews had no weapons like Jabin's. They were peaceful farmers and shepherds.

For twenty years Jabin's men caused the Hebrews trouble. It was not safe for the Hebrews to work in their fields or travel the roads alone.

God heard their cries for help, and He felt sorry for them.

Memory Verse
But I cry to you for help, O Lord . . . my prayer comes before you.
Psalm 88:13

Deborah Goes to Battle

Bible story from Judges 4:4-16; 5:1-31.

A wise woman named Deborah was a Hebrew judge. She liked to sit in the shade of a palm tree while she talked to the people who needed her help.

One day God told Deborah to send for a man named Barak. When Barak came, Deborah told him, "God says He wants you to call ten thousand Hebrew men to make a great army. You are to fight King Jabin."

Barak was afraid of King Jabin's army. And he wondered how ten thousand shepherds and farmers would be able to win a battle against Jabin's iron chariots.

Barak said, "The people know and trust you, Deborah, not me. If you will go into battle with me, I will go. But if you won't go, I won't go."

"I will go with you," Deborah said. "But when the battle is won, there will be no glory for you because you didn't trust God. God will let a woman win the battle instead."

Barak did what Deborah told him. He called together ten thousand Hebrew men to make an army. They had no iron chariots to ride in like King Jabin's men. The Hebrews marched into battle on foot. And Deborah went with them.

God told Deborah and Barak to take the army to Mount Tabor. When King Jabin's army heard where the Hebrew army was going, they followed them.

The two armies met near the Kishon River. As they started to fight, God sent a great rain storm.

The river flooded and the ground turned to sticky mud. King Jabin's chariots were soon stuck. His mighty army grew frightened, and his soldiers tried to run away. The general of his army ran into a tent and was killed by a woman named Jael.

The Hebrew army won the battle. Deborah and Barak sang a song to praise God for His help. Now the Hebrew people would be safe for a while.

Memory Verse
I will sing to the Lord, I will sing.

Judges 5:3a

God Helps Gideon

Bible story from Judges 6—7.

Gideon was a farmer. The wheat he had grown was almost ready to make into bread. "I'll hide the grain from my enemies," Gideon said. Enemies had taken his grain before.

So Gideon and his people prayed. They asked God for help. "Please show us what to do," they said.

An angel came to Gideon and told him, "God will help you fight the enemies. He will show you what to do."

Gideon blew a trumpet and called all the men in his land. "Come to fight our enemies," he said. "God will show us what to do."

Many men came to fight. But God told Gideon, "There are too many men. Send the scared men home." God talked to Gideon again. "You still have too many men," God said.

"Tell the men to drink from the river. Count the men who use their hands to drink the water. Use only these men to fight."

Gideon counted three hundred men. He sent the other men home.

Then God told Gideon to fight the enemies at night.

Instead of swords and spears, each man went to battle with a trumpet and a clay jar with a burning torch inside.

While the enemies were sleeping, the men blew their trumpets. They also broke the jars. The enemy soldiers were afraid and ran away.

Gideon and his people were safe again. God had answered their prayers. God had shown them what to do.

Memory Verse
Seek and you will find; knock and the door will be opened to you.
Matthew 7:7b

Samson the Strong

Bible story from Judges 13:1-7; 16:4-30.

In the days when the Philistines were the Hebrews' enemies, an angel visited a Hebrew woman. "You will soon have a son," the angel said. "And if you leave his hair long, he will be strong. God will give him the job of protecting his people."

When the baby was born, he was named Samson. His parents never cut his hair. And just as the angel promised, Samson grew into a very strong man.

Samson's girlfriend, Delilah, promised to help the Philistines capture Samson. "What's the secret of your strength?" Delilah asked him one day.

Samson laughed and wouldn't tell her. She tried tying him up with strong straps, and then strong ropes. But he broke them easily. She braided his hair into her loom, but he jumped up just as strong as ever.

Finally he said, "If my hair is ever cut, I will become as weak as any other man." So Delilah cut his hair the next time he took a nap. And just as he had said, his great strength left him.

As Samson slept, Delilah called to the Philistines hiding in her house. Then she shouted, "Samson, the Philistines are here!"

Samson jumped up, but his great strength was gone. The Philistines grabbed him and blinded his eyes. Then they gave Delilah some money and took Samson away to their city.

They put him in prison and chained him to a grinding stone. But they didn't know that as his hair grew longer, he grew stronger.

One day, the Philistines had a big party.

They brought Samson out to show to all the people. Everyone laughed at him, because they thought he was weak.

But when they chained Samson between two pillars, he pushed the pillars over and the roof fell down. Everyone in the building was killed. Samson punished the Philistines for everything bad they had done to him and to his people.

Memory Verse
Be on your guard; stand firm in the faith; be men of courage; be strong.

I Corinthians 16:13

Ruth Honors Naomi

Bible story from the Book of Ruth.

Ruth and Naomi started off on a long trip. They were going to the place where Naomi had been born. Naomi had left her home many years before with her husband and sons.

Now Naomi's husband was dead. Her sons were dead too. She had only Ruth to help her. Ruth had been the wife of one of Naomi's sons.

Ruth loved Naomi as her own mother.

As they walked along, Naomi said to Ruth, "You don't need to leave your home to go on this trip with me."

Ruth hugged Naomi and told her, "I want to stay with you and help you. Your family will be my family. And your God will be my God."

Naomi and Ruth finished their trip. Naomi's old friends were surprised to see her. They were glad she had Ruth to take care of her.

Ruth and Naomi were too poor to buy food. Ruth went to a field of grain. She picked up the leftover grain so she and Naomi could use it to make flour for bread.

Boaz owned the field of grain. Boaz told Ruth, "You may take all the grain you need because you are so kind to Naomi."

One day, Naomi told Ruth to ask Boaz for his help. So Ruth did. Boaz wanted to help Naomi and Ruth because he loved Ruth.

Ruth loved Boaz too. Ruth and Boaz got married. They asked Naomi to live with them so they could take care of her. Later, Ruth and Boaz had a baby.

Naomi's friends said to her, "God has been good to you. He has given you a fine family."

Memory Verse
Honor your father and your mother.

Exodus 20:12a

Hannah Thanks God

Bible story from I Samuel 1:1—2:19.

Hannah was a woman who loved God. But Hannah was very sad because she did not have any children.

One day she went to God's house. It was a big tent called a tabernacle.

Hannah told God how sad she was. She prayed, "Dear God, please give me a little boy. If You do, I will raise him to love You and be Your helper always."

Hannah kept praying for a long time. A priest named Eli saw her and said, "Don't be sad. God will answer your prayer."

Hannah didn't feel sad anymore. She went back home. Soon God did answer Hannah's prayer! God gave her a little baby boy. Hannah named the baby Samuel. How Hannah loved her baby! She fed him and made little clothes for him. She took good care of him. Hannah was thankful to God for saying yes to her prayer.

As Samuel grew bigger, Hannah remembered her promise to God. Hannah told Samuel about God's house. She told him about Eli, the priest. She helped Samuel learn to obey God and be God's helper.

Then the time came for Samuel to be a helper at God's house. Hannah took Samuel to the tabernacle.

Hannah said to Eli, the priest, "Remember
how I prayed for a son? Look! God gave him
to me. Now my son will always be God's helper."

Then Hannah gave thanks to God for answering her
prayers.

Memory Verse
Be glad and rejoice. Surely the Lord has done great things.

Joel 2:21b

Samuel Listens

Bible story from I Samuel 3:1-19.

Samuel was a young boy. He lived in God's house and helped Eli, the priest. One night when Samuel was in bed, he heard a voice call his name. Samuel ran to Eli. "Here I am. You called me?" said Samuel.

The old priest said, "I didn't call you. Go back to bed, Samuel." So Samuel went back to bed.

Again the voice called. "It must be Eli," Samuel thought. But no, Eli had not called him.

When the voice called a third time, Eli knew it was God calling Samuel's name. Eli told Samuel, "Next time, tell God you will listen."

Samuel went to bed. Again God called him. Samuel said, "I'm listening, God." Samuel listened to everything God said. And Samuel kept on listening to God and obeying Him as he grew up.

Memory Verse
I will listen to what God the Lord will say.

Psalm 85:8a

God Chooses David

Bible story from I Samuel 16:1-13.

When Samuel grew up, he became a prophet. He told the people about God's plans. He also told King Saul, but King Saul did not obey God anymore.

God told Samuel, "I have chosen a new king. I will show you who the new king will be. Go to Bethlehem and find a man named Jesse. I have chosen one of his sons." So Samuel went to Bethlehem, just as God told him to.

One by one, Samuel saw seven of Jesse's sons. He said, "The Lord has not chosen any of these. Do you have any more sons?"

"Yes," Jesse said. "The youngest one, David, is taking care of the sheep."

When young David came to see Samuel, God said, "He is the one who will be king." So Samuel anointed David with oil.

Memory Verse
"For I know the plans I have for you," declares the Lord.
Jeremiah 29:11a

David Plays for King Saul

Bible story from I Samuel 16:8-23.

David was the youngest in his family. He was a shepherd for his father's sheep. Sometimes David played the harp and sang.

Samuel was the Lord's prophet. One day he came to the town where David lived. He had come to choose someone to serve God in a special way.

Samuel looked at David's brothers. Samuel said to David's father, "God has chosen one of your sons to be king. But I don't see the one He has chosen. Are these all the sons you have?"

The father said, "There is one more. It is David, the youngest. He is taking care of the sheep."

Samuel said, "Ask him to come here."

When David came, God spoke to Samuel. God said, "I have chosen David."

Samuel poured some oil on David's head. Then David knew that God had chosen him to do something special.

Later, King Saul felt sad and gloomy. What could help him feel better?

Someone said, "David can help you. He plays the harp well. His music will make you feel better. And the Lord is with him. You should ask him to come here."

So King Saul asked David to come. God showed David how to help the king. Whenever King Saul felt sad and gloomy, David played his harp. When King Saul heard the happy music, he felt better right away.

Memory Verse
Don't let anyone look down on you because you are young, but set an example.

I Timothy 4:12a

David Fights a Giant

Bible story from I Samuel 17.

David's older brothers were soldiers in the army of God's people. They went to fight an enemy army. David watched his father's sheep. He kept them safe from lions and bears.

One day David's father told him, "Take some food to your brothers."

When David found his brothers, they weren't fighting the enemy. All of the soldiers were afraid!

"What is the matter?" David asked.

"You'll see," his brothers said.

Soon an enemy soldier walked out. He was a giant named Goliath. "I want a man to fight me!" he shouted to the army of God's people. But none of the soldiers moved.

David said to the soldiers, "We should not be afraid of this giant. God is on our side. He will help us."

King Saul heard about the brave young man. He sent for David. "You are just a boy," King Saul said.

145

"I will fight the giant," David said. "God helped me kill a lion and a bear. I know He will help me kill this giant."

David picked up five stones for his sling. Then he went out to meet Goliath. The giant had a sword and a spear.

Goliath laughed when he saw David. "You are just a boy!" said Goliath.

David said, "You are brave because of your sword and spear. But I am brave because I trust God."

David put a stone in his sling. He pulled back the sling and let it go. The stone flew out of the sling and hit the giant in the head. Goliath fell down dead.

Then the soldiers chased away the enemy army. David had shown them how to be brave. David trusted God to help him.

Memory Verse
The Lord is my helper; I will not be afraid.

Hebrews 13:6b

Jonathan Helps His Friend David

Bible story from I Samuel 18:1-16; 19:1-7.

After David killed Goliath, King Saul asked David to live at his palace. David played the harp and sang for Saul. His music helped the king feel better.

The king had a son named Jonathan. Jonathan and David became best friends. They took walks and hunted together. Jonathan gave David his coat as a present. "We will always be friends," they said.

Then David helped King Saul by fighting in a war. David was a good soldier. He helped King Saul's army win.

The people loved David. They sang songs about him in the streets. "The king has won many battles," they said. "But David has won the most!"

The king was angry when he heard the songs. "My people like David better than me," he said. He felt angry at David.

One day, David was playing the harp for the king.
King Saul threw a spear at David to hurt him. David
was afraid and ran away. Jonathan heard what his
father had done to David. "I need to help my friend,"
he thought. Jonathan went to talk to David. "David,
hide in a safe place," he said. "I will talk to my father
about you."

Then Jonathan went to his father, the king. "David has
done many good things," Jonathan said. "He has not tried
to hurt you, Father. So you shouldn't try to hurt him.
That would be doing wrong."

King Saul listened to his son, Jonathan. He promised not to hurt David again.

Jonathan went to David's hiding place. "David, it is safe for you to come back now," he said. So David went back to be the king's helper. Jonathan was glad he could help his friend David.

Memory Verse
A friend loves at all times.

Proverbs 17:17a

David and the Sleeping King

Bible story from I Samuel 26.

King Saul broke his promise to David. The king wanted to kill him. David tried to hide with his men. He moved from town to town. He hid in caves and in woods. But he was never safe from King Saul for very long.

One day someone told King Saul where David was. The king and his army marched after David. At last they climbed a hill near David's hideout.

All the soldiers were tired. "We'll rest here tonight and find David in the morning." said King Saul. The king's soldiers set up camp. Saul lay down to rest. His spear and water jug were next to him. A man named Abner lay beside the king to keep him safe. Soon everyone fell asleep.

Later, David and one of his men came along. They saw the king's men all sound asleep! "Let's go closer to the king," said David. So they walked right up to the sleeping King Saul

"I will kill the king," David's friend said. "Then he will not hurt you anymore."

"No!" said David. "Saul is the king. We should not hurt the leader God chose. God will punish him for the wrong he has done."

David and his friend took the king's spear and water jug. They went to a nearby hill and David shouted, "Abner, wake up! You have not taken good care of your king. Someone could have hurt him."

King Saul woke up and saw that his spear and water jug were gone.

Saul knew that David could have killed him. "I'm sorry I chased you, David," Saul said.

David said, "I could have killed you tonight, but I would not hurt the king God has chosen. Now may God keep me safe too."

Saul said, "May God bless you. You will do great things." Then David went away with his men. And King Saul went home.

Memory Verse
Obey your leaders and submit to their authority.

Hebrews 13:17a

David Asks for Help

Bible story from I Samuel 30:1-20.

David and his men came back from battle. They found a terrible surprise. Enemies had burned their town! Enemies had stolen their sheep and cows! Enemies had taken their families away!

David and his men cried and cried. They cried until they had no more tears. Then the men grew so angry with David, they wanted to throw stones at him. David did not know what to do next.

David told God he was in trouble. "Shall I chase the enemy?" he asked, and God said yes.

So David and his men went after the enemy. They found a man who was a servant of the enemy soldiers. They gave him food and he took them to the enemy's camp.

David's army attacked and got their families and animals back. God answered David's cry for help.

Memory Verse
He cares for those who trust in him.

Nahum 1:7b

The New King

Bible story from I Samuel 31; II Samuel 2:1-7, 11; 5:1-2;
Psalm 18:48-50.

When David was a boy caring for sheep, God said he would be king someday. But years went by and Saul was still king. Yet David still trusted and obeyed God.

One day King Saul was killed in a battle. He and his son Jonathan both died. David was sad to hear about King Saul. David cried about his friend Jonathan.

God's people did not have a king anymore, so the people came

to David. They asked him to be the new king.
David knew God's promise had come true.

David was the king for many years. He honored God
and followed His laws. And David wrote songs to praise God.
These songs are called psalms. Together, the people sang them.
"We praise You, God, for taking care of us. We will always trust
You and obey You."

Memory Verse
Teach me your way, O Lord, and I will walk in your truth.

Psalm 86:11a

David's Psalm

Bible story from Psalm 145:1-12.

King David wrote songs. They were called psalms. This is one of King David's psalms:

I will tell everyone how great You are, my God and King. Every day I will thank You. I will praise You forever and ever. You are worthy of praise. You are greater than anything else.

People should tell their children and their children's children the mighty things You do. I will tell everyone how great You are! Everyone will sing of Your goodness.

You are loving and forgiving. You are slow to get angry. You are good to everyone. All Your people will give You thanks. Everyone will know how great You are and how wonderful Your kingdom is.

Memory Verse
Great is the Lord and most worthy of praise.

Psalm 145:3a

King David Helps a Lame Prince

Bible story from
II Samuel 4:4; 9.

Jonathan had a son named Mephibosheth. When Mephibosheth was five years old, he lived at the palace with King Saul.

King Saul and Prince Jonathan died in battle. Then everyone at the palace was afraid. The boy's nurse said, "We must run and hide! If we don't, enemy soldiers may hurt you!"

Mephibosheth and his nurse ran out the door. The nurse picked up the little boy so that they could run faster. But Mephibosheth fell and hurt his legs.

The soldiers never found Mephibosheth. He was safe, but his legs never got better. The prince grew up to be lame. It was hard for him to walk.

When David became king, he thought about his friend Jonathan. "Is anyone alive in Jonathan's family?" he asked. A servant told King David about Mephibosheth. David sent his servants to find Jonathan's son.

Mephibosheth was a grown-up now, but he was afraid to see David. Mephibosheth still thought someone might want to hurt him.

But David was very happy to see the son of his friend Jonathan. "Don't be afraid," said David. "Your father was my friend. I promised to help him always, but he is dead. So, now I want to help you. I want you to live near my palace and eat your meals at my table."

Mephibosheth brought his family to live near the palace of David. Mephibosheth was just like one of the king's sons. David had kept his promise to Jonathan by being kind to his son. He told Mephibosheth, "I will always take care of your family."

Memory Verse
Share with God's people who are in need.

Romans 12:13a

Worship Time

Bible story from I Chronicles 29:10-21.

King David and God's people came together to praise God. They had given many gifts to build a temple for God. They wanted to worship God before the building work began. God had chosen the king's son Solomon to be in charge of building the temple.

First King David prayed, "We praise You, Lord. You are great and powerful. Everything we have comes from You. We thank You. We praise Your name.

"We are happy to give these gifts to You. Help my son, Solomon, obey You. Help him build Your temple."

Then King David said to God's people, "Praise the Lord your God."

So all the people bowed low. They all praised God together.

Memory Verse
Come, let us bow down in worship, let us kneel before the Lord our Maker.

Psalm 95:6

King Solomon's Request

Bible story from I Kings 1:32-40; 2:12; 3:3-15.

King David was very old. A new king was needed for God's people. So Solomon, David's son, was anointed king.

But Solomon was worried. Would he be able to rule well? He knew he needed God's help.

God talked to Solomon in a dream: "Ask Me for anything you want."

Solomon knew what he wanted. "Lord, please give me wisdom to be a good king," he said.

God was pleased with Solomon. "You could have asked to be rich. You could have asked for a long life. But you asked for the best thing. I will give you wisdom. I will also make you rich. And if you keep obeying Me, you will have a long life, too."

Memory Verse
If any of you lacks wisdom, he should ask God . . . and it will be given to him.

James 1:5

Solomon's Temple
for God

Bible story from I Kings 4:29—7:51.

Solomon had become king of God's people. God gave Solomon wisdom to be a great king. God also gave Solomon important work to do. Solomon was to build a beautiful temple where all the people would come to worship God.

Wise King Solomon worked very hard to plan how the temple would be built. Solomon wanted God's temple to be the most beautiful in the world.

First, Solomon wrote to the king of another land, "Your trees
have the finest wood. I would like to buy your wood for the
temple." The other king was happy to help Solomon.

Solomon sent good workers to cut down the trees. They were
very careful to do the job just right. *Crash!* went the tall trees
falling to the ground.

Other workers cut the wood into boards for the walls of the
temple. They were very careful to do the job just right too.
Buzz! went their saws as they cut the wood. Solomon needed
many more good workers.

Big stones were used for the floor. These were brought to the temple and put into place. Other workers made tall pillars for the doorway. Still more workers made lampstands of gold. All were careful to do their jobs just right.

God helped all of the workers to do their best work for His beautiful temple.

Finally the temple was finished. The people thanked God for His help. God had given the workers wisdom to do a good job.

It was good to work for the Lord. Now they had a beautiful place to worship Him.

Memory Verse
Be very careful, then, how you live—not as unwise but as wise.

Ephesians 5:15

Day of Thanksgiving

Bible story from II Chronicles 5-7; I Kings 8:54-61

The temple was finally built! Solomon held a special day of thanksgiving. *Clang!* Cymbals clashed. *Tra-la!* The choir sang happily. *Ta-da-dum!* Trumpets sounded. How good it was to worship God in the beautiful new temple.

A thick cloud filled the temple. That was God's way to show He was there.

Solomon said to all the people, "There is no god like our God!

He has always been with us. He gave us this land to live in. He gives rain and good food. He is here in this house we have built for Him."

Solomon had a feast of thanksgiving. Then the king prayed to God. "Thank You for all You have done! Please help us to obey You always. We want to follow You."

Memory Verse
Accept, O Lord, the willing praise of my mouth, and teach me your laws.

Psalm 119:108

King Solomon Disobeys God

Bible story from I Kings 11—12.

Once God promised young Solomon any gift he wanted. Solomon had asked God for wisdom. Solomon wanted to be a good king. God gave Solomon wisdom, and riches, too. Solomon's part was to obey God's commandments.

Solomon was wise when he obeyed God and built Him a beautiful temple. He was wise when he obeyed and worshiped only the one true God.

God's people were happy and at peace, and Solomon became famous all over the world.

But Solomon's wives were from many different lands. His wives did not worship the one true God. Some of them worshiped idols.

"Please, King Solomon," they said, "build us palaces to worship our idols, too."

Solomon knew that worshiping idols was not obeying God's commandment.

God said people should worship only Him. But Solomon built the place to worship idols anyway. Soon Solomon did something else that wasn't wise. To please his wives, Solomon himself began to bow down to the idols. God was very angry.

God said, "Solomon, because you disobeyed Me, I will take part of your kingdom away from your son when you die."

After Solomon's death, Solomon's son and another man both tried to be king of God's people. There were many wars and battles. The country was split into two countries. Each country had its own king.

God's people were unhappy again because Solomon did not use the wisdom God gave him. Solomon disobeyed God.

Memory Verse
Do not let me stray from your commands.

Psalm 119:10b

God Guides Elijah

Bible story from I Kings 16:29—17:6.

Ahab was a king who did not obey God. Ahab did not worship God. He worshiped an idol named Baal.

Elijah was a man who loved God. God made Elijah a prophet and gave him a message for King Ahab.

Elijah said to Ahab, "You have done many wicked things. So God will not let it rain in your kingdom until I say so."

King Ahab was angry. He wanted to hurt Elijah. But God kept Elijah safe. God told Elijah to hide near a brook. Even though it did not rain, Elijah had water to drink. God sent birds with food for Elijah. Elijah followed God's way and was safe.

Memory Verse
Believe in the Lord Jesus, and you will be saved.

Acts 16:31a

God's Wonderful Gifts

Bible story from I Kings 17:7-16.

It had not rained for a long time. There was a famine in the land. Elijah was still hiding near a brook, but it was dried up. God told Elijah to go to a faraway town. God said, "A widow there will help you."

Elijah saw the widow gathering sticks. Elijah said, "Please bring me some water and a piece of bread."

The widow said, "I don't have any bread. I just have a little

flour and oil. When they're gone, my son and I will die."

Elijah said, "Don't be afraid. Make some bread for us. God will not let you run out of flour or oil."

The widow did what Elijah said. Elijah, the widow, and her son had food every day. God took care of them during the famine.

Memory Verse
Every good and perfect gift is from above.

James 1:17a

God Answers Elijah's Prayer

Bible story from I Kings 17:17-24.

Elijah was staying with a widow and her son. One day the widow's son got very sick and died. The widow was very sad. She asked Elijah, "Why did God let my son die?"

Elijah said, "Give me your son." Elijah carried the boy upstairs and put him on the bed.

Then Elijah began to pray. He knew God would listen. Elijah said, "Lord God, please let this little boy live again!"

God heard Elijah's prayer and made the boy live again. Elijah took the boy to his mother. The widow said to Elijah, "Now I know you are a man of God. God has answered your prayer!"

Memory Verse
Call to me and I will answer you.

Jeremiah 33:3a

Fire on Mount Carmel

Bible story from I Kings 18:16-39.

After three years without rain, God sent Elijah to King Ahab. Elijah said, "You have sinned by worshiping idols instead of worshiping God. Tell all the people and the prophets of Baal to meet me on Mount Carmel."

When everyone was together on Mount Carmel, Elijah said, "How long will you worship Baal instead of the one true God? Today you will find out who the one true God is! Then you will know you should follow only Him."

Elijah told all the false prophets to build an altar and put an offering on it. Elijah said he would build an altar and put an offering on it, too.

Elijah said, "You can call to your idol. I will call on the name of the Lord. The one who answers by sending fire to burn up the offering—that is the true God."

The false prophets did what Elijah said. They called on the idol Baal all morning. But no fire came to burn the offering.

Elijah said, "Shout louder! Maybe Baal can't hear." The false prophets called on Baal until it was nearly dark. But Baal didn't answer. No fire came down.

Elijah said to the people, "Come with me." Elijah poured water over the altar he had made. Then Elijah called on God. Elijah said, "Oh Lord, answer me. Then these people will know You are the true God."

God answered Elijah. The fire came down. It burned up the offering. It burned up the altar. It even burned up the water.

When the people saw this, they knew they had been wrong. They were sorry they had worshiped idols like Baal. Then they fell down and said, "The Lord—He is God! The Lord—He is God!"

Memory Verse
For all have sinned and fall short of the glory of God.

Romans 3:23

God Comforts Elijah

Bible story from I Kings 19:1-18.

On Mount Carmel God had shown Ahab and the people that He was the real God. Then God had sent rain as He promised. But wicked Queen Jezebel was angry. She wanted to kill Elijah.

Elijah was afraid. He ran into the desert and sat under a tree. He was so tired from running that he soon fell asleep.

But God took care of Elijah. An angel came and woke him up. The angel brought food and water. After Elijah ate, he climbed up a mountain and hid in a cave.

Elijah felt alone and afraid. He thought he was the only one left who believed in God. God wanted to help Elijah feel better.

God said, "Go out and stand on the mountain."

As Elijah stood on the mountain, God sent a strong wind. The wind broke the rocks into pieces. Then God sent an earthquake. The ground shook and shook. And then came a fire that crackled and burned.

Elijah was in the middle of the wind, earthquake, and fire. But Elijah wasn't hurt. God took care of him.

Then Elijah heard a whisper. It was God! God was talking to Elijah in a whisper.

God told Elijah what to do. God said that a man named Elisha would be his new helper. God told Elijah that he didn't have to be alone anymore.

Elijah listened to God's voice. Elijah knew God would always take care of him. Elijah didn't feel so alone and afraid anymore. He went down the mountain to find his new helper, Elisha.

Memory Verse
Come to me, all you who are weary and burdened, and I will give you rest.

Matthew 11:28

King Ahab Wants a Vineyard

Bible story from I Kings 21:1-19; Exodus 20:13, 15, 17.

King Ahab had everything he needed. But he was selfish. King Ahab wanted more, and he didn't like to be told no.

King Ahab saw a nice vineyard. The vineyard belonged to Naboth. Ahab wanted Naboth's vineyard.

"Your vineyard is near my home," King Ahab said to Naboth. "I would like to have it. I will buy it from you. Or I will give you another one."

But Naboth said, "No, thanks. I can't let you have it. God would not be pleased. It belongs to my family. We have owned it a long, long time. It is good land and it grows fine grapes. We don't want any other land or your money."

The king was angry. He went home and would not eat. He just lay on his bed. Jezebel was Ahab's wife. She came in and asked, "Why are you angry? Why won't you eat?"

"Naboth wouldn't sell me his vineyard," Ahab told Jezebel. "I still want that vineyard!"

Jezebel sent a letter to some men: "I want you to tell some lies about Naboth so he will be killed." The men did what Jezebel told them to do.

Then Jezebel told Ahab, "Naboth is dead. Now the vineyard is yours."

God sent His prophet Elijah to Ahab. Elijah told Ahab, "God's commandments say you shall not murder and you shall not steal. You did not obey God's commandments. God will punish you."

Memory Verse
You shall not steal.

Exodus 20:15

Elisha Is Chosen

Bible story from I Kings 19:19-21, II Kings 2:1-15.

Elijah was God's prophet. He did what God told him to do. But Elijah was getting old. God said, "I want you to come live with Me, Elijah. Find a man named Elisha. I have chosen him to be My new prophet."

Elijah found Elisha working in a field. Elisha was plowing with oxen. Elijah threw his cloak around Elisha's shoulders. Elisha knew that this meant he had been chosen to be Elijah's helper.

Elisha said, "I will come with you. But first, I must tell my family good-bye." Then he followed Elijah and watched and learned how to be a good prophet.

One day Elijah said, "God told me to go to another city. You stay here."

But Elisha wanted to be with Elijah. Elisha said, "I will not leave you. I will go where you go."

Elijah and Elisha came to a river. They needed to get to the other side.

Elijah hit the river water with his cloak. The water divided to the left and right. Then the two men walked across on a dry path!

Elijah knew he was going to be with God soon. He asked Elisha, "What can I do for you before I leave?"

Elisha said, "I want God's power so that I can do His work the way you do."

Elijah said, "If you see me leave, you will know that God will give you His power."

Suddenly a fiery chariot appeared and a strong wind lifted Elijah up into the sky to be with God. Elisha watched him go.

Elijah's cloak fell to the ground and Elisha picked it up. Then he went back to the river and hit the water with the cloak. The water parted as it had for Elijah and he walked across. Elisha knew God's power was with him. Now he was ready to do God's work.

Memory Verse
Always give yourselves fully to the work of the Lord.

I Corinthians 15:58b

Micaiah Tells What Is True

Bible story from II Chronicles 18; Exodus 20:16.

Once there were two kings. King Jehoshaphat loved and obeyed God, but King Ahab didn't.

Jehoshaphat went to see Ahab. "I want to take over an enemy city," said Ahab. "Will you help me?"

"Before I can answer, I will need to know what God wants us to do," said King Jehoshaphat.

So Ahab called his prophets, and four hundred prophets came. Ahab asked them, "Shall we fight to get the city?"

The prophets knew what King Ahab wanted them to say. And they didn't want to make him angry at them. So they didn't tell the truth. They all said, "Go ahead. God will give you the victory. The city will be yours."

But Jehoshaphat didn't trust these prophets. He asked, "Is there another prophet of God you can call? I would like to hear what he has to say."

"Micaiah is a prophet of God," Ahab said to Jehoshaphat. "But I do not like him. He never tells me what I want to hear."

"Well, I want to hear what Micaiah says," said Jehoshaphat. Jehoshaphat wanted to hear what an honest prophet of God would have to say. So Ahab sent for Micaiah.

The messenger who went to get Micaiah told him, "Be smart. Just tell Ahab what he wants to hear."

But Micaiah said, "I must tell the truth because that is what God wants me to do."

Micaiah told the two kings, "You can go to the enemy city and attack it, but you, King Ahab, will be killed. The other prophets did not tell you the truth."

King Ahab was angry. He threw Micaiah in prison. Then King Ahab attacked the enemy city. And he was killed just as Micaiah had said he would be.

Memory Verse
Do not lie to each other.

Colossians 3:9a

God Answers a
King's Prayer

Bible story from
II Chronicles 20:1-25.

King Jehoshaphat was a good king. He trusted God and tried to do right. He helped his people trust and obey God too.

One day some men brought upsetting news to the king. They said, "A big enemy army is coming this way! They want to have a war with us."

The king said, "Tell my people to come to Jerusalem. We will go to the temple together and pray. We will ask God to help and protect us. I know He will do it."

The king's people hurried to the temple. King Jehoshaphat stood up and prayed. He said, "Dear God, a big army is coming! We do not have enough soldiers to fight such a great battle. You are a great God. Please help us."

All the people—even the boys and girls—prayed with the king. Then one of the priests said, "God has told me to tell you: 'Do not be afraid. The battle is not yours to fight, but God's. Go out to meet the enemy tomorrow morning. But don't worry, you will not have to fight them. God will take care of everything.' "

Next morning, King Jehoshaphat and his army marched out to meet the enemy. They marched until they came to a big hill. They knew that the enemy soldiers were camped on the other side.

When they marched to the top of the hill, what a surprise was in front of them! The enemy army was there, but they were all dead! They had fought and killed each other.

The king and his people had not expected this answer to their prayer. God took care of everything. They didn't have to fight at all! They were glad they trusted God to do what was best.

Memory Verse
The Lord will indeed give what is good.

Psalm 85:12a

Elisha Helps a Widow in Need

Bible story from II Kings 4:1-7.

A poor widow went to see Elisha. She asked him, "What can I do? I am poor and owe money I can't pay. I'm afraid my sons will have to become slaves to the man I owe money."

Elisha knew God would help. He asked her if she still owned anything. The widow said, "I only have a little jar of olive oil."

Elisha said, "Ask your neighbors for all the empty jars you can borrow. Then fill them with oil from your jar."

The widow's sons borrowed many jars. Then the widow picked up her little jar of oil and began filling them. The little jar of oil didn't become empty until all of the big jars were full.

Elisha said, "Now sell the oil and pay the man what you owe him. Then use the money that's left to buy food for your family." God had shown Elisha how to help the widow when she was in need.

Memory Verse
Dear children, let us not love with words . . . but with actions.

I John 3:18a

Naaman Gets Help from a Servant Girl

Bible story from II Kings 5:1-15.

Naaman was the leader of a big army. But Naaman was sick with leprosy. No doctors knew how to help him get well.

A girl who worked as a servant in Naaman's house wanted to help. She told Naaman's wife, "My master should go and talk to God's prophet, Elisha. God will show Elisha how to help my master."

When Naaman heard the girl's idea, he asked his king if he could go to see Elisha. The king wanted Naaman to get well too, so he sent a letter to the king of Elisha's country. The letter said, "Please make Naaman well."

Elisha heard about the letter. He sent a message to the king that said, "Send Naaman to me." But when Naaman got to Elisha's house, Elisha wouldn't come out to see him. Instead, Elisha sent his servant outside to give Naaman a message.

Elisha's message said, "Go wash in the Jordan River seven times and God will make you well."

Naaman was angry. This was no way for Elisha to treat an important man like him! But Naaman's servants said, "Please do what Elisha says."

So Naaman went to the muddy Jordan River. He dipped himself in the water once, twice, three times, four times; but nothing happened.

Naaman dipped himself in the water five, six, seven times.
And when he came up for the seventh time, the leprosy was
gone. He was well!

Naaman went back to thank Elisha. He said, "Now I know
that your God is the only true God." Naaman thanked God for
making him well and for the servant girl who told him God
could help.

Memory Verse
Serve one another in love.

Galatians 5:13b

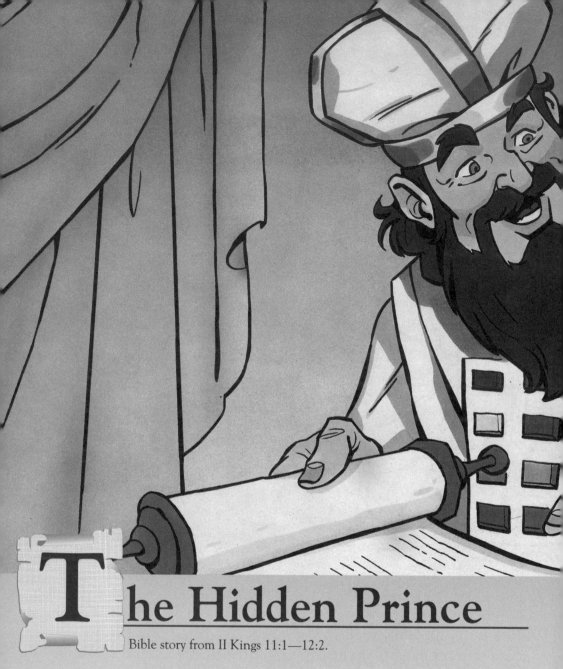

The Hidden Prince

Bible story from II Kings 11:1—12:2.

Joash was a Hebrew prince, but his father, the king, died while Joash was young. His grandmother was an evil woman and she wanted to be queen. When she heard her son was dead, she sent soldiers to kill all of her grandsons.

Joash's Aunt Jehosheba took him to the temple to hide. The soldiers looked and looked for Joash, but they didn't think to look in the temple.

Joash lived in the temple for six years. One of his uncles was a priest there. He taught Joash how to read the Bible scrolls, and how to please God. With the help of his uncle, Joash learned to love God. Joash said, "Someday when I am king, God's people will come to worship at the temple again."

When Joash was seven years old, he became the new king. And God helped him be a good one.

Memory Verse
Remember your leaders, who spoke the word of God to you.
                                                    Hebrews 13:7a

Worshiping at God's House

Bible story from II Chronicles 29:20—30:27.

When Hezekiah became king, it bothered him that his people no longer worshiped God. King Hezekiah said to the people, "It is wrong for us to forget about God. Let's gather together and worship Him."

So everyone went to the temple and worshiped. The people prayed, "Dear God, we are sorry for doing wrong things. We promise to learn about You and to praise You."

Then King Hezekiah and his people worshiped God with music. Some played their harps. Some played their trumpets. Others hit their cymbals together.

The people also sang songs to worship God. They sang words like: "Shout for joy to the Lord, all the earth. Serve the Lord with gladness; come before Him with joyful songs. Enter His gates with thanksgiving and His courts with praise; give thanks to Him and praise His name."

Later, King Hezekiah sent letters to all his people who lived far away. He told them to come and worship at God's house too.

Many people came to the temple. They also asked God to forgive them for doing wrong things, and they sang songs and played music. The priests read from God's Word and told the people about God. Then the people gave God their offerings and prayers.

King Hezekiah and his people worshiped at God's house for seven days. It was such a happy time that they didn't want to go home. So they worshiped God for seven more days. God was pleased that His people had come to the temple to worship Him.

Memory Verse
Worship the Lord with gladness; come before him with joyful songs.
Psalm 100:2

221

Hezekiah's Prayer

Bible story from II Kings 20:1-11.

King Hezekiah was very sick. "God told me you will die soon," the prophet Isaiah told him.

This news made the king sad. After Isaiah left, the king prayed, "God, please make me well."

Then Isaiah came back. He said, "God heard your prayer, King Hezekiah. He told me to tell you that He will make you well."

The king was still worried, so he asked, "How can I be sure?"

Isaiah answered, "Every day the sun makes a shadow go down the palace steps. But today God will make the shadow go up the steps."

The sick king watched the palace steps to see what would happen. And just as Isaiah said, God made the shadow go up the steps instead of down. And God made the sick king well because the king had remembered to ask God for help.

Memory Verse
For everyone who asks receives; he who seeks finds; and to him who knocks, the door will be opened.

Matthew 7:8

God's Word Lasts

Bible story from Jeremiah 36.

God said to the prophet Jeremiah, "Write these words on a scroll: 'My people have not obeyed me. I will let their enemies destroy them if they do not choose to obey Me.'"

Jeremiah told his helper Baruch to write God's words on a scroll and read the scroll to God's people. Some of the people were afraid. They knew God's Word was true.

A man read God's words to the king. The king became angry and burned the scroll in a fire. He did not think God's Word was true.

God told Jeremiah to write the words again on another scroll. God said, "This country will not last, but my Word will last forever."

Memory Verse
The word of our God stands forever.

Isaiah 40:8b

Three Brave Men Show Faith in God Bible story from Daniel 3.

A long, long time ago, King Nebuchadnezzar built a shiny gold idol. It was ninety feet high and nine feet wide.

Then he sent word throughout the land that all leaders should worship the idol. When the music played, the leaders bowed and worshiped the statue . . . all except Shadrach, Meshach, and Abednego. They refused to bow before the idol.

The three men said, "We will not bow down. The God we serve said, 'Don't worship anything but Me!' And He is able to help us no matter what you do."

King Nebuchadnezzar grew very angry. He ordered his soldiers to throw the three men into a fiery furnace!

Immediately, the king's order was carried out. Then an amazing thing happened. When the king looked inside, he saw the men walking around! Their clothes were not burned. They were not hurt in any way.

"Didn't we tie three men up and throw them into the fire?" the king asked. "Look, I see four men walking around."

The king shouted, "Shadrach, Meshach, and Abednego, come out! Your God has saved you!"

"I'm giving an order," the king said. "No one can say anything against the God of Shadrach, Meshach, and Abednego. No other god can save people the way their God can."

Memory Verse
You shall have no other gods before me.

Exodus 20:3

Daniel Obeys God

Bible story from Daniel 6.

Daniel loved God and prayed to Him three times each day. He also worked hard for the king. He was a trusted servant, so King Darius wanted to put Daniel in charge of the whole kingdom.

But the other leaders were jealous and wanted to get Daniel in trouble. "Make a law," they told the king, "that no one can pray except to you for thirty days."

The king thought this sounded fine so he signed the law with his royal pen. Anyone who did not obey would be thrown into the den of lions'.

But Daniel went home and did as he always did. He prayed to God. Nothing could stop him from obeying God's law. His enemies heard him and reported Daniel to the king.

The king was sad that these crafty men saw Daniel breaking the law. But even the king couldn't change the law, so Daniel was thrown into the lions' den.

The king said, "Daniel, God be with you." He didn't know what else to do. All night he wondered, "Is Daniel all right?" Early in the morning, he went to check the den.

"Did God take care of you?" he asked. How glad he
was when Daniel replied, "God sent His angel to shut
the lions' mouths. I am not hurt."

The king was filled with joy. "Get Daniel out of the den,"
he said. "Daniel's God is the One to whom we should
pray. He saved Daniel from the lions."

Memory Verse
Do what is right and good in the Lord's sight.

Deuteronomy 6:18a

Nehemiah Prays

Bible story from Nehemiah 1:1—2:9.

Nehemiah heard some bad news about the people who had gone back to Jerusalem. "God's people are having trouble. The city is in bad shape. Even the city walls are broken down."

Nehemiah prayed, "O Lord, we are Your people, but we did not obey You. So You made us leave our homeland. Now You have told us to go back home again. Please help us rebuild the city of Jerusalem."

God heard Nehemiah's prayer. Nehemiah asked the king of Persia if he could go back to Jerusalem to help rebuild the city walls. The king said yes.

Nehemiah had a plan to rebuild the city, and God's people said that they would help him. Nehemiah was happy that God had answered his prayer!

Memory Verse
The Lord will hear when I call to him.

Psalm 4:3b

God's People Did Not Quit

Bible story from Nehemiah 2:11—4:23; 6.

God sent Nehemiah to Jerusalem. The city's enemies had torn down its walls. Nehemiah said, "God will help us rebuild the walls. We won't give up." And he gave each person a job to do.

The enemies of God's people tried to stop the work. They laughed at the people. But God's people did not give up. They kept on building the city walls. Then the enemies said, "We will fight you if you don't stop working!" This scared God's people.

Nehemiah told them, "Don't be afraid. God wants us to rebuild Jerusalem's walls. He will help get the job done. You must work with one hand and hold your sword with the other hand."

The people decided to be brave and keep on working. Their enemies didn't attack after all. And finally the city walls were finished.

Memory Verse
Let us not become weary in doing good

Galatians 6:9a

Ezra Says Obey

Bible story from Nehemiah 8.

The people of Israel gathered together at the new walls of Jerusalem. They asked Ezra, the priest, to read to them from God's Word. He read in a loud voice, "Praise the Lord. He is our great God. Obeying His Word makes us happy."

But hearing God's Word made some of the people cry. They knew that they had not obeyed God's Word and now they were sorry. "Don't cry," Ezra said. "Now that you understand God's Word, you can obey it and be happy."

It had been a long time since the people had heard God's Word. So Ezra stood by the new city walls and read God's Word out loud for seven days. The people came to listen. Then they all thanked God for His help.

The people said, "From now on we will listen to God's Word, and we will obey His commands. Then God's Word will make us happy."

Memory Verse
Blessed . . . are those who hear the word of God and obey it.
Luke 11:28b

Esther Saves Her People

Bible story from the Book of Esther.

It was a sad day for Mordecai. King Xerxes, the ruler of Persia, was looking for a wife. The most beautiful girls in the land were being called to the palace to meet him.

Mordecai's cousin, Esther, was like a daughter to him. She had lived with him since she was a little girl. Now the king wanted to meet her. And Mordecai didn't want Esther to leave.

He knew that the king would fall in love with Esther as soon as he met her. She was very beautiful and kind.

"Don't tell the king you are a Hebrew," he warned Esther. "There are many people in this land who do not like us because we worship the one true God."

Mordecai watched as Esther walked toward the palace. He wondered if he would ever see her again. "I want Esther to be happy," he told himself. "But I will miss her."

Mordecai was right. The king did fall in love with Esther. He chose her to be his queen. Mordecai missed his cousin, but he knew that she was happy.

One day Mordecai heard some terrible news! A bad man named Haman was planning to have all of God's people killed. He and his friends had tricked the king into signing a law. It said on one special day it would be okay to kill God's people and steal the things they owned.

Mordecai put on torn clothes and ashes to show he was upset. When Esther heard, she sent a man to ask him what was wrong.

Mordecai said, "Go to the king and tell him about Haman. See if the king can help us. Even you, Esther, won't be safe if Haman's plans work out. He must be stopped."

Esther was afraid. She knew that even the queen couldn't see the king whenever she wanted to. It was against the law for anyone to see the king without being invited. If he was unhappy she came, he could have her put to death.

Esther prayed for courage. She fixed her hair and put on her best dress. Then she headed off to see her husband, the king.

King Xerxes was surprised to see his wife. "Esther looks lovely," the king said to himself. "But why would she risk her life by coming to see me without being called?" The king raised his scepter to show Esther that she was welcome to speak to him.

"My Lord," Esther said with a bow, "I would like to invite you and Haman to have dinner with me."

"We would be happy to come," the king replied.

The king and Haman enjoyed the dinner Esther planned. And when she asked, they both agreed to come to dinner again.

But the next time they came, Esther told the king about Haman's plan to kill all the Hebrews, even her.

The king was very angry. He made a new law to help save God's people. And then he had Haman hanged.

With God's help, Queen Esther saved her people. And Mordecai was very proud of her.

Memory Verse
Our God is a God who saves.

Psalm 68:20a

Jonah and the Big Fish
Bible story from Jonah 1-3.

One day God told a man named Jonah to go to the city of Nineveh. Jonah was a preacher. God wanted him to preach to the people of Nineveh and tell them that God was unhappy with the wrong things they were doing.

That's too hard, thought Jonah. *I don't want to go to Nineveh. Those people are our enemies.* So he found a boat that would take him far away, as far away from Nineveh as he could get.

But after the boat headed out to sea, a big storm came up. The thunder rumbled and crackled. The lightning flashed. Even the sailors were afraid. They started to throw things off the boat to make it lighter. But nothing helped.

The captain went to find Jonah. " I know you are a preacher. Ask your God to save us!" he said.

Then Jonah said, "Throw me into the sea and the storm will stop. This trouble is my fault." Jonah knew that God had sent the storm because he was running away from what God wanted him to do.

So the sailors threw Jonah into the sea. And he went down, down, down into the dark, cold water. But Jonah didn't die. God sent a big fish to save him. The big fish opened its mouth and swallowed Jonah in one big gulp.

Jonah stayed inside the fish's belly for three days. It was dark and smelly and very uncomfortable, but Jonah was happy. He was still alive!

Jonah thought about what had happened. He knew that God had saved him, so Jonah prayed. He thanked God for saving his life. He told God he was sorry for running away. And he told God he would obey Him and go to Nineveh.

After three days, God had the big fish swim close to land and spit Jonah onto the shore.

Then God said, "Jonah, obey Me and go to Nineveh. Tell the people there what I said."

So Jonah obeyed God and went to Nineveh. The people there listened to what he had to say. They told God they were sorry for the wrong things they had done and God forgave them.

Jonah learned an important lesson. He learned that you can't run away from God. Obeying God makes life a lot happier. Jonah was thankful that God forgave him and gave him a second chance to obey.

Memory Verse
I desire to do your will, O my God; your law is within my heart.
Psalm 40:8

Isaiah Tells of Jesus

Bible story from Isaiah 7:14; 9:1-7.

Isaiah was a prophet of God. He lived almost seven hundred years before Jesus was born. God told Isaiah many things about the future. Isaiah wrote down the things God told him. Then Isaiah told God's people what God had said.

Isaiah said that one day God would send His people a new king. This new king would be the best king they ever had. He would be a relative of King David. This new king would be called Wonderful Counselor, Mighty God, Everlasting Father, and Prince of Peace.

He would be born to a woman God chose, and His name would mean "God is with us." His kingdom would be a kingdom of peace that would last forever.

When Jesus was born, these words of Isaiah came true. Jesus is the Prince of Peace God promised to send to the world. If we love and obey Him, we are part of His kingdom of peace.

Memory Verse
For to us a child is born, to us a son is given.

Isaiah 9:6a

The
NEW
Testament

A Promised Son

Bible story from Luke 1:5-25, 57-80.

Zechariah was a priest in the temple. He and his wife Elizabeth wanted children but they had none. Now they were very old and didn't believe they would ever have a family.

One day Zechariah was working in the temple when he saw an angel. The angel said, "You and Elizabeth will have a baby. His name will be John. When he grows up, he will help people get ready for the coming of God's Son."

Zechariah said, "How can this be?"

"God sent me to tell you," the angel said. "But because you did not believe me, you will not talk until the baby is born."

God's promise came true. Baby John was born and Zechariah could talk again. Zechariah and Elizabeth thanked God for their son. They thanked God that it was time to get ready for God's Son to come.

Memory Verse
The Father has sent his Son to be the Savior of the world.

I John 4:14a

The Angel's Message

Bible story from Luke 1:26-56.

Mary was a young woman who lived in a town called Nazareth. One day an angel came to give Mary a message from God.

At first Mary was afraid. But the angel said, "Do not be afraid. God is going to do something wonderful for you. You will have a baby boy. And you will name Him Jesus. Jesus will be the Son of God."

"I believe your message," said Mary. "I will do what God wants me to do."

Mary hurried to tell her cousin Elizabeth the angel's message.
God helped Elizabeth know that Mary's baby would be the
Savior of all people.

Then Mary sang a song of praise to God. She thanked God for
all the wonderful things He does. She thanked God for
sending His Son, Jesus, to be the Savior.

Memory Verse
I tell you the truth, he who believes has everlasting life.

John 6:47

The Shepherds' News

Bible story from Luke 2:1-20.

Mary and Joseph were on their way to a town called Bethlehem. The ruler of the land had made a law that said all people should go to their hometown to be counted. It was a hard trip for Mary. She was going to have a baby. God's Son would soon be born.

When Mary and Joseph got to Bethlehem, the town was full of people. There was no room for Mary and Joseph to stay in the inn.

Mary and Joseph went to stay in a stable. Soon Mary's baby was born. Mary wrapped the baby in strips of cloth. She made a bed for Him in a manger. The baby's name was Jesus.

That same night some shepherds were watching their sheep in the hills near Bethlehem. Suddenly, the shepherds saw an angel. A bright light was shining around the angel. The shepherds were afraid.

The angel said, "Do not be afraid. I have wonderful news! It is happy news for everyone. Our Savior has been born in Bethlehem. He is Christ the Lord. Go to Bethlehem and find Him. He is wrapped in strips of cloth. You will find Him lying in a manger."

Then there were many angels in the sky. All of them were singing praises to God for sending Jesus the Savior. Then they went back to heaven.

The shepherds hurried to Bethlehem. They wanted to see the Savior. After the shepherds saw Jesus, they praised God for sending His Son. They told everyone they saw that Jesus the Savior had been born.

Memory Verse
Today in the town of David a Savior has been born to you.

Luke 2:11a

Gifts for a King

Bible story from Matthew 2:1-12.

"We must keep following the star," said the wise men as they rode their camels across the desert. "The star will lead us to the special child. He is the new king of God's people."

The wise men were making a long trip to find the new king. They wanted to worship Him. They wanted to give Him gifts of gold, incense, and myrrh.

After a long trip the wise men came to a big city. "Where is the new king?" the wise men asked the people. "We want to worship Him."

The people didn't know anything about a new king. Their leader was King Herod. And King Herod was angry when he heard the news. He asked his helpers where the new king had been born. His helpers said, "God's Word says that He would be born in Bethlehem."

King Herod told the wise men a lie. He said, "Go and find the new king for me. Then come and tell me where He is. I want to worship Him too."

So the wise men left the king's palace and followed the star again. It led them to a house in Bethlehem. There they saw little Jesus sitting on His mother's lap. They knelt down and worshiped Him. Then they gave Him their gifts of gold, incense, and myrrh. These gifts showed their love for Jesus.

In a dream, God told the wise men not to go back to King Herod and tell him where Jesus was.

They knew King Herod would try to hurt little Jesus so that Jesus could not be the next king. But God would not let King Herod hurt His Son, Jesus.

The wise men headed home a different way. They were glad they had come to worship Jesus and to give Him gifts to show their love.

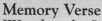

Memory Verse
Worship the Lord your God, and serve him only.

Matthew 4:10b

Seeing the Savior

Bible story from Luke 2:21-38.

Mary and Joseph loved baby Jesus. They knew He was a special gift from God. So they made a trip to God's temple to thank Him for sending them Jesus.

An old man named Simeon was at the temple that day. God had made him a promise. God told Simeon that he would live long enough to see God's Son. So Simeon was always watching for this special child. When he saw Jesus, God told him his wait was over.

Simeon took baby Jesus in his arms. He thanked God for letting him see this special child. "I have seen Your Son as You promised," Simeon prayed. "You sent Him to be the Savior. He will teach many people about You, and He will help everyone."

Someone else noticed Jesus too. Anna was an old woman who lived at the temple. When she saw Jesus in Simeon's arms, she thanked God too. She said, "He is the One who will save us!"

Memory Verse
We know that this man really is the Savior of the world.

John 4:42b

God Protects Jesus

Bible story from Matthew 2:13-15, 19-23.

Mary, Joseph, and little Jesus lived in Bethlehem. Jesus was sent by God His Father to be the Savior of the world.

One night God sent an angel to talk to Joseph in a dream. The angel said, "Hurry Joseph! You must take Mary and Jesus to Egypt. King Herod is looking for Jesus because he wants to kill Him."

So the family left right away. They stayed in Egypt until one night God sent an angel to talk to Joseph again. The angel told him, "You can go back to your own country now. King Herod is dead, so Jesus will be safe now."

So Joseph took Mary and Jesus home to the town of Nazareth. God had kept His Son, Jesus, safe so that someday He would be the Savior of the world.

Memory Verse
The plans of the Lord stand firm forever.

Psalm 33:11a

Jesus at Home

Bible story from Luke 2:39, 40, 52; Matthew 13:55, 56;
Deuteronomy 6:4-9.

God chose Mary and Joseph for the special job of raising His
Son. They weren't rich or important people, but God knew
that they could give His Son, Jesus, what He really needed—
lots of love!

Jesus grew up in the town of Nazareth. Mary took care of the
house and Joseph worked as a carpenter. The men of Nazareth
taught their sons how to earn a living. So Joseph taught Jesus
how to be a carpenter. He showed Him how to work with tools.

The men of Nazareth also taught their families how to love and honor God. Joseph taught God's Word to his family. He said, "You must love the Lord your God. You must love Him with all your heart."

Jesus' family helped Him learn the things He needed to know. They helped Him grow strong and tall. They helped Him show love to other people and to His Heavenly Father.

Memory Verse
For God said, "Honor your father and mother."

Matthew 15:4a

Young Jesus at the Temple

Bible story from Luke 2:41-52.

Mary and Joseph lived far from the temple. So they only went there once a year.

Jesus was twelve years old. He went with Mary and Joseph. They had to walk almost a week. Many other people walked with them. The people were glad to get to Jerusalem. They could see the temple right away. It was a beautiful place.

Jesus went to the temple with His family. They worshiped God at the temple. They sang and prayed to God. They gave their offerings to God.

Then Mary and Joseph started back home. They walked all day. They thought Jesus was safe with another family in their group.

That night Mary and Joseph looked around. But they couldn't find Jesus. They said, "We must go back to Jerusalem."

They went back to look for Jesus. They found Him at the
temple. Jesus was listening to wise teachers. He asked them
some questions. And He answered their questions. Mary went
over to Jesus, "Why have You done this to us? We have looked
everywhere for You."

"Why did you look so hard?" asked Jesus. "Didn't you know I
would be here? This is My Father's house." Jesus was talking
about God. Jesus knew that God was His Father.

Jesus liked to be at God's house. But He obeyed Mary and Joseph. He went back to Nazareth with them.

God was pleased with Jesus. People were pleased with Jesus too.

Memory Verse
I rejoiced with those who said to me, "Let us go to the house of the Lord."

Psalm 122:1

Jesus at School

Bible story from Luke 4:16; Deuteronomy 6:4, 5; Mark 6:1-4.

Jesus went to the synagogue in Nazareth. That's where He and His family went to worship God. He went to school there, too, on weekdays.

The teacher at the synagogue loved God. He read to his students from Bible scrolls. "You shall love the Lord your God with all your heart," he read. Jesus learned to read and write the Bible words.

Jesus learned many things at home, too. He learned about God and the Bible from Mary and Joseph. And He learned to help around the house and how to build things out of wood.

When He grew up, Jesus remembered the things He learned. He taught them to many other people. Jesus was the best teacher anyone ever had.

Memory Verse
Let the wise listen and add to their learning.

Proverbs 1:5a

John Tells of Jesus

Bible story from John 1:19-34.

Jesus had a cousin named John. He started preaching before Jesus did. John told people that Jesus was coming soon. John said that God wanted him to tell everyone to get ready for Jesus and to stop doing wrong things.

Many people who listened to John felt sorry for their sins. So John baptized these people in the river.

Some men asked John, "Who are you?"

"I am not the Savior," said John. "But I am here to tell you that He is coming."

The next day John saw Jesus walking toward him. John said, "Here is the person I have been telling you about. This is Jesus, the Savior. He will save us from our sins."

John said, "I know Jesus is God's Son, and I want everyone to know it. Jesus IS the Son of God!"

Memory Verse
For God so loved the world that he gave his one and only Son.

John 3:16a

Special Helpers

Bible story from Mark 3:13-19; Luke 6:12-16; Matthew 10:1-8.

Jesus was very busy teaching people and helping them with their problems. He wanted someone to help Him. So He asked twelve men to be His special helpers. He called the men His disciples.

When Jesus taught people, the disciples listened too. They helped Jesus with His work. They learned many things from Him. One day Jesus said to His disciples, "I want you to tell people that God loves them. And God will give you the power

to make sick and sad people better. Since I have helped you, you can go and help other people, too."

The twelve disciples said, "We want to show God that we love Him. So we will go help other people just as You taught us to do."

Memory Verse
For we are God's workmanship, created in Christ Jesus to do good works.

Ephesians 2:10a

Jesus Is Our Best Friend

Bible story from Matthew 19:13-15; Mark 10:13-16.

The crowds that followed Jesus weren't just grown-ups. Some children came to see Jesus too. Their families wanted Jesus to pray for the children and bless them.

Jesus' helpers knew He was busy. "Leave Jesus alone," they said. "He is too busy with grown-ups. He doesn't have time for children."

The boys and girls were sad. But then they heard Jesus say, "Wait! Let the little children come to Me. God loves boys and girls. The kingdom of heaven belongs to everyone who is like these children."

Jesus smiled at the boys and girls. He put His arms around them. He said, "Grown-ups must love God. They must trust Me as children do."

Memory Verse
Let the little children come to me.

Mark 10:14b

A Captain Has Faith in Jesus

Bible story from Matthew 8:5-13.

Once there was an army captain who led one hundred soldiers. He was a very important man. His soldiers always obeyed what he told them to do.

The captain also had many servants. They obeyed the captain too. The captain was very kind to his soldiers and servants.

One day a servant of his became very sick. The captain wanted

to help his servant. Another servant told the captain that Jesus was in their town.

The captain knew that Jesus helped people. He had faith in Jesus and went to find Him. The captain believed Jesus could make the sick servant well.

When the captain found Jesus, he said, "Sir, my servant is very sick. I know that You can make him well. Will You help my servant?" The captain had faith in Jesus.

"Yes, I will help," Jesus said. "I will come to your house."

But the captain told Jesus, "I am not good enough to have You come to my house. All You have to do is say that my servant will get well, and it will happen."

Jesus was happy about what the captain said to Him. He said to the people there, "I have never met anyone with so much faith in Me."

The captain believed Jesus. When the captain got home, his servant was well. Jesus made the servant well because of the captain's faith in Him.

Memory Verse
I will put my trust in him.

Hebrews 2:13a

Jesus Helps a Sick Man

Bible story from Mark 2:1-12; Luke 5:17-26.

Four men took their sick friend to see Jesus. The man could not walk so his friends carried him on a bed mat. They wanted the man to see Jesus because they believed Jesus could help him walk.

Jesus was teaching in a house. Many people were listening to Him. The four men took their friend to the house, but the house was so full the four men couldn't even get their friend inside the door.

"I know what we can do," said one man. "Let's go up on the roof. We can make a hole in it and lower our friend down into the house to see Jesus."

So the men carried their friend to the roof. They made a hole that could be fixed later. Then they tied ropes to the bed mat and slowly and carefully lowered their friend down through the hole.

Jesus saw the man coming down on the mat. He saw the man's friends up on the roof. He was glad that they believed in Him. Jesus smiled at the man on the mat. "Your sins are forgiven," He said.

Some of the people in the house grew angry. "Only God can forgive sins," they said. They didn't believe Jesus was God's Son.

Jesus wanted them to know who He was. He wanted them to know what He could do. The people could not see if the man's sins were forgiven. But they could see Jesus' special power if He healed the man.

"Stand up," Jesus said to the man. "Pick up your bed and walk." Right away the man got up and rolled up his bed mat. And then he began to walk!

"Thank You, Jesus," said the man. And all the way home, the man thanked God.

How surprised all the people were! Everyone thanked God. They knew Jesus had special power. He could forgive sins and make people well. He could do it because He is God's Son.

Memory Verse
The Lord is full of compassion and mercy.

James 5:11b

Jesus Stops a Storm

Bible story from Mark 4:35-41.

Jesus and His helpers got into a boat. The helpers started to row, and Jesus lay down in the boat and soon fell asleep.

Soon the wind began to blow. It made the waves get bigger and bigger. Water began to splash into the boat and fill it. Jesus' helpers were afraid of the storm. They didn't know what to do. Everyone was sure the boat would sink.

"Wake up, Jesus!" the helpers called. "Teacher, don't You care if we drown?"

Jesus spoke. "Stop," He said to the wind. "Quiet! Be still!" He said to the waves. The wind stopped and the waves went away.

Everything was quiet on the lake. Jesus looked at His helpers. "Why were you afraid?" Jesus asked them. "Don't you trust Me?"

The helpers saw Jesus' special power. "Even the wind and waves obey Him," the helpers said.

Memory Verse
Do not let your hearts be troubled. Trust in God; trust also in me.
John 14:1

Jesus Makes a Sad Family Happy

Bible story from Mark 5:21-24, 35-43.

One day a very sad man came to Jesus. His name was Jairus. Jairus was a leader in the synagogue. The synagogue was a place where Jewish people went to worship God.

"Please help me, Jesus," Jairus said. "My little girl is dying. If You will just come and touch her, I know that she will be well. Then we can be happy again."

Jesus said that He would go with Jairus to see the little girl. There were many other people wanting to talk to Jesus too. They crowded around Him, so He couldn't walk very fast.

As they came near Jairus's house, some men came running up to Jairus. They cried, "It's too late. Your little girl is dead. Jesus doesn't need to come now."

Jairus was so sad. He believed that Jesus could help his little girl, but now it seemed to be too late.

"Don't be sad, Jairus," Jesus said. "Just believe in Me." They walked on to Jairus's house. There they found many people crying.

"Don't cry," Jesus told them. "She is only sleeping." This made the people laugh at Him. Jesus went into the girl's room and walked over to her bed. He held her hand and said, "Get up, little girl!"

The little girl started to breathe and opened her eyes. Then she sat up and got out of bed.

When the people saw her, they stopped crying and were happy. Jairus and his wife smiled too. Then they gave the little girl something to eat "Thank You, Jesus! Thank You!" the happy parents said.

Jesus was glad He helped Jairus. Jesus liked helping people with their problems.

Memory Verse
The Lord is close to the brokenhearted and saves those who are crushed in spirit.

Psalm 34:18

Jesus Helps a Deaf Man

Bible story from Mark 7:31-37.

Once there was a deaf man. He could not hear anything. He could not talk well, either. This man's friends had to give him special help.

One day the deaf man's friends took him to see Jesus. They asked Jesus to help the man. They knew Jesus loved people who needed special help.

Jesus took the man aside and talked to the man. He touched the man's ears and tongue. Then Jesus said, "Open up!"

Suddenly the man could hear sounds. He could talk, too. The man and his friends were glad that they had come to Jesus for help.

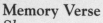

Memory Verse
Show proper respect to everyone.

I Peter 2:17a

Jesus Helps Bartimaeus

Bible story from Mark 10:46-52; Luke 18:35-43

Jesus was walking from town to town. Many people were walking with Him.

There was a blind man begging outside the city of Jericho. His name was Bartimaeus. Bartimaeus couldn't see anyone, but he could hear people.

One day Bartimaeus heard a crowd coming. He asked the people what was going on. "Jesus is coming by," the people said.

Right away Bartimaeus called out to Jesus. He had heard that Jesus could heal people. "Jesus, please help me!" called the blind man.

Some people nearby said, "Be quiet, Bartimaeus."

But the blind man would not be quiet. He called out louder, "Jesus! Please help me, Jesus."

Jesus stopped and said, "Tell that man to come here." Bartimaeus heard Jesus' kind voice. He couldn't wait to get to Jesus. He hurried toward the kind voice.

Jesus asked the blind man, "What do you want Me to do for you?"

"Oh, Jesus, I want to see," said Bartimaeus.

Jesus said, "You believe in Me. So now you are well." Right away Bartimaeus could see. He was not blind anymore!

Bartimaeus began to follow Jesus, thanking God for Him. Bartimaeus knew Jesus had special power from God, and Jesus had used it to make him well.

Many other people saw what Jesus did. They thanked God for Jesus too.

The people learned more about Jesus each day. They learned that Jesus can help everyone who believes in Him. Jesus can do it because He is God's Son!

Memory Verse
Finally, be strong in the Lord and in his mighty power.

Ephesians 6:10

Jesus Solves a Big Problem

Bible story from John 5:1-9

In the city of Jerusalem there lived a man who had been crippled a long time. The man could not walk. All day long he lay on his bed mat by the Pool of Bethesda waiting for help. He hoped that God would send an angel to touch the water of the pool and give the water power to heal him. But no one at the pool would help him get into the water.

Then one day Jesus came to visit the Pool of Bethesda. He saw the sick man lying on his bed mat beside the pool. He knew how long the man had been crippled and He felt sorry for him. Jesus had the power to help the man, so He went over to talk to him. "Do you want to get well?" Jesus asked him.

"Oh, yes," the man answered. "I want to walk very much, but no one will help me get into the water when it starts to move."

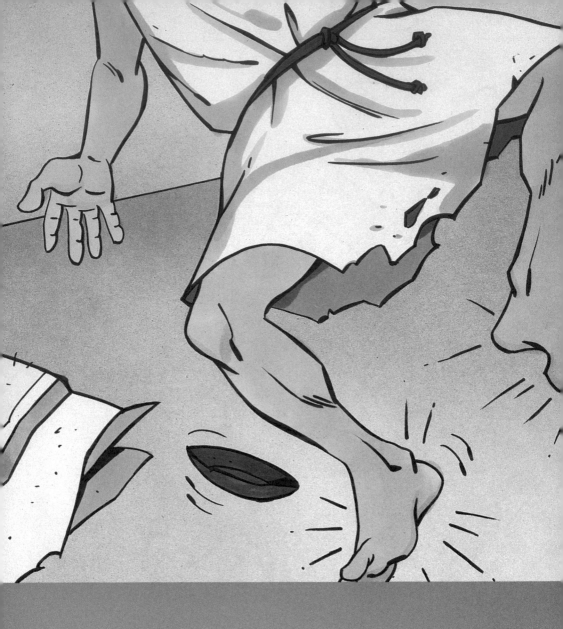

Then Jesus said to him, "Get up! Your legs are well. Pick up your bed mat and walk!"

The man looked very surprised. But he stood up on his feet. His legs did feel strong! Then he picked up his bed mat and started walking around. He felt very, very happy. Other people who saw him felt happy, too. Jesus' power had solved the man's problem.

"Thank You, Jesus," said the man. Then he hurried away to go tell other people how Jesus had helped him and made him well.

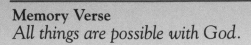

Memory Verse
All things are possible with God.

Mark 10:27b

Jesus Uses A Boy's Lunch

Bible story from
John 6:1-14.

Jesus wanted to talk to His helpers alone. So He took them up a hill, but soon many other people followed them. These people came from towns all around. They had seen Jesus make people well. They wanted to hear Him talk about God.

Jesus loved the people and wanted to help them. So He began to teach them about God.

After a while, it was time for supper, but there was no town close to them. The people began to get hungry.

Jesus talked to one of His helpers. "Philip, where can we buy food for all of these people?"

Philip said, "It would take too much money. We can't buy food for all these people. We should send them home."

Then Andrew came to Jesus. He was also one of Jesus' helpers.

Andrew said, "Here is a boy with a lunch he is willing to share. But he only has five small rolls of bread and two small fish. That won't be enough food for everyone. There are more than five thousand people here!"

Jesus said, "Have the people sit down on the grass." Then He thanked God for the food and broke the bread and fish into pieces.

Jesus' helpers passed out the pieces of bread and fish, and there was enough food for everyone!

When everyone was finished, Jesus told His helpers, "Gather the leftover food." So the helpers picked up the leftovers. They filled twelve baskets!

The people knew that Jesus was special. Now they saw more of His special power. With one little boy's lunch, Jesus fed more than five thousand people!

Memory Verse
So whether you eat or drink or whatever you do, do it all for the glory of God.

I Corinthians 10:31

Mary and Martha Ask Jesus for Help
Bible story from John 11:1-44.

Mary and Martha were Jesus' friends. Their brother, Lazarus, was Jesus' friend too. Jesus liked to go and visit their home in the town of Bethany.

One day when Jesus was far away, Lazarus became sick. Mary said, "Jesus could make Lazarus well. But He is not here to help us."

Martha said, "We can send someone to tell Jesus about Lazarus. I know Jesus will come and help our family." So they sent someone to tell Jesus that their brother, Lazarus, was very sick.

But before Jesus could walk to His friend's house, Lazarus died. Mary and Martha and their friends were sad. They wrapped Lazarus in graveclothes and buried him in a cave-tomb.

When Jesus finally arrived, Martha ran to meet Him. "Oh, Jesus!" she cried. "I wish You had been here sooner; then Lazarus would not have died. But I know that You can still help us."

Jesus said, "Don't worry, Martha. Trust in Me."

When Mary saw Jesus, she too said, "Oh, Jesus! If You had come sooner, Lazarus would still be alive."

Jesus asked the two sisters to take Him to the burial place. Jesus said, "Roll away the stone." Then he prayed, "Dear God, thank You for always hearing My prayers."

Then Jesus cried, "Lazarus, come out!"

And Lazarus came out of the tomb. He was still wrapped in the graveclothes.

Jesus said, "Take those things off him." So they did and there stood Lazarus—well and alive again!

Mary and Martha were so happy. They thanked their friend Jesus for helping their family. They thanked Jesus for making their brother well again.

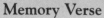

Memory Verse
Pray for each other so that you may be healed.

James 5:16b

Praying for Good Things

Bible story from Luke 11:1; Matthew 6:9-13; 7:7-11.

Jesus always took time to pray. He prayed to God, His Heavenly Father. God always answered Jesus' prayers. God gave His Son the good things He needed when Jesus prayed.

One day as Jesus was praying, His helpers saw Him. They waited until He was done; then they said to Him, "Jesus, please teach us how to pray." So Jesus did. He told them what a good prayer was like.

Jesus said, "Pray like this: Heavenly Father, Your name is holy. Help us to do what You want. Give us the food we need today. Forgive us for doing wrong. Help us forgive other people who do wrong things to us. Keep us from wanting to do wrong."

Jesus promised His helpers that God would give them the good things they needed if they asked Him to. Jesus said, "Ask and it will be given to you; seek and you will find; knock and the door will be opened to you. For everyone who asks receives; he who seeks finds; and to him who knocks, the door will be opened."

Jesus also said, "If a hungry child asks for bread, his father will not give him a rock to eat. A good father will give his child good things. God is your good Heavenly Father. He will give you the good things you need, if you ask Him."

Memory Verse
Ask and it will be given to you.

Matthew 7:7a

Two Builders

Bible story from Matthew 7:24-29.

One day Jesus told this story about two men.

A wise man built a house on hard ground. Then one night it rained hard. The wind blew on the house too. But the wise man was safe because his house on the hard ground stood straight and strong.

A foolish man built a house too, but he built his house on the sand. Then one night there was a big storm. The wind blew and it rained hard. The foolish man was not safe because his

house was built on sand, and it soon fell down with a crash!

People who obey Jesus are like the wise man. They will be safe when problems come because they trust in Jesus.

People who do not obey Jesus will end up very sad, because they trust in things that can't really help them. They are like the man whose house fell down.

Memory Verse
If you love me, you will obey what I command.

John 14:15

Helping Jesus

Bible story from Matthew 10:42; 25:31-40.

Jesus told His friends:

"Someday I will sit on a throne. Everyone will come before Me. I will say to the people who love Me, 'I was hungry, and you gave Me food. I was thirsty, and you gave Me water. I was a stranger, and you were friendly to Me. I was sick, and you took care of Me. I had poor clothes, and you gave Me good clothes.'

"My friends will say, 'When did we do those things, Jesus?'"

"I will answer, 'When you were kind to others, it was the same as being kind to Me.'"

Memory Verse
Always try to be kind to each other.

I Thessalonians 5:15b

Keeping God's Day Holy

Bible story from Matthew 12:9-15; Exodus 20:8-11.

It was the sabbath day. God's commandment said the sabbath should be a holy day to worship Him. Jesus wanted to worship God. He was going to a place called a synagogue. This was where God's people went on the sabbath day to worship and learn about God.

The rulers of the synagogue did not like Jesus. "Let's see if Jesus breaks any of our rules for the sabbath. Then we can get Him in trouble," said one of rulers.

Another ruler pointed to a poor man with a crippled hand. "Maybe Jesus will heal that man's hand," he said. "That's against the rules. Healing the man would be work and no work is allowed on the sabbath."

The rulers went to Jesus and asked, "Is it right to heal someone on the sabbath day? Isn't that work?"

Jesus answered, "If one of your sheep fell in a hole on the sabbath, wouldn't you lift it out? A person is more important than a sheep. So it is right to do good on the sabbath."

Jesus said to the poor man with the crippled hand, "Put your hand out." The man put his hand out and suddenly, he could move his fingers and wave his hand. Jesus had healed him!

Jesus knew the right way to keep the sabbath day holy. He worshiped God. And He helped other people.

Memory Verse
Remember the Sabbath day by keeping it holy.

Exodus 20:8

A Young Man Loves His Money

Bible story from Matthew 19:16-22;
Exodus 20:3; Deuteronomy 6:5.

A rich young man asked Jesus a question. "Teacher, I want to live with God forever. What good thing should I do?"

Jesus said, "If you want to live, obey God's commandments."

"Which ones?" the rich man asked.

Jesus told him, "Do not kill. Do not steal. Do not lie. Honor your father and mother. And love your neighbor as much as you love yourself."

"I obey these commandments," the young man said. "What else must I do?"

Jesus said, "If you want to be perfect, sell what you own and give your money to poor people. Then your riches will be in heaven, and you can come and follow Me."

Jesus knew the man loved money more than he loved God. If the man gave his money away, he wouldn't have to think about it anymore or spend time deciding what to buy with it.

Jesus wanted him to give his money to the poor because the man had so much and the poor had so little. Giving his money away would show he loved God more than he loved his money.

The rich man didn't want to hear what Jesus said. He walked away. He loved his money too much to give it up—even to obey God.

Keeping Promises

Bible story from Matthew 21:28-31.

One day Jesus told this story: A man had a vineyard. He said to his first son, "Please pick grapes for me today."

But the son said, "No, I don't want to work today."

Then the father said to his second son, "Please pick grapes for me today." The second son promised he would help his father.

Later, the first son changed his mind. He said, "I should obey my father." So he went to the vineyard and worked all day.

The second son also changed his mind. "I don't feel like working after all," he said to himself. So this son did not keep his promise to help his father.

Then Jesus asked the people with Him, "Which son did the right thing?"

The people answered, "The first son. The second son did not keep his promise."

Memory Verse
The Lord detests lying lips, but he delights in men who are truthful.
Proverbs 12:22

The Best Way

Bible story from Mark 10:35-45.

James and John said to Jesus, "We want to sit by You in heaven. Will You let one of us sit next to Your throne on the right and the other on Your left?"

The other disciples were angry. James and John had asked Jesus for the very best places.

Jesus said to them, "Most people try to be a boss over others. Everyone wants the best for himself. You should think of others first. The best way is to be a helper to others."

"I have shown you how to do this. Though I am God's Son, I didn't come to get things for Myself. I came to help people and even give My life for them."

Memory Verse
Honor one another above yourselves.

Romans 12:10b

A Poor Woman Gives Her Offering

Bible story from Mark 12:41-44.

One day Jesus was in the temple. Some of His disciples were there too. Jesus sat near the offering box. He and His disciples watched people walk by it.

People dropped money into the box as they came into the temple. Back then, there was no paper money, only coins. The coins made a noise when they were dropped into the box.

 Plunk! went the little coins. *Clunk!* went the big coins. Everyone heard the noise the coins made.

A rich man walked into the temple. He put some big coins in the offering box. *Clunk, clunk, clunk!* The rich man smiled. He was glad his money made so much noise. Everyone could hear how much money he gave.

Jesus saw many people come and go. They all put money in the offering box. Big coins, small coins. Loud clunks, soft plunks. Many people did not give their money because they loved God. They gave it to show off and make other people think they were important.

Then a very poor woman came into the temple. Her husband was dead, so she was a widow. She dropped two small coins into the box: *Plunk, plunk!*

She knew it did not sound like much money. But she loved God. So she gave Him all the money she had.

Jesus told His disciples to look at her. "Many rich people have come here," He said. "They have put in a little of their money. But this woman gave God her best. She gave Him everything she had."

Memory Verse
Each man should give what he has decided in his heart to give.
II Corinthians 9:7a

Jesus Reads the Scriptures

Bible story from Luke 4:16-22.

One day Jesus went back to Nazareth. During worship at the synagogue, the people said, "Jesus, will You read from God's Word for us today?"

Jesus read from Scripture: "God has sent Me to preach good news to poor people. He has sent Me to set prisoners free, to help blind people see, and to help all people in need."

Then Jesus told the people, "Today these Scripture words have

come true." Jesus meant that He was the One God had sent to preach the good news and help people in need.

The people were surprised. They did not believe that Jesus was God's Son. They said to each other, "Jesus is Joseph's son. He grew up here in Nazareth. He is just a man like us."

But Jesus really is God's Son. The Scriptures tell about Him.

Memory Verse
Your word is a lamp to my feet and light for my path.

Psalm 119:105

The Good Samaritan

Bible story from Luke 10:30-37.

Jesus often used stories to teach people what God wanted them to do. One day He told this story.

A Jewish man was walking along a lonely road. Some robbers were hiding behind the rocks beside the road. They jumped out and hit the man many times until he was almost dead. Then they took his money and clothes and left him lying by the road.

Soon a priest from God's temple came walking by. He saw the hurt man, but he did not stop to help.

Next a Levite from the temple walked past. The Levite saw the hurt man, but he walked on by too.

Then a Samaritan man walked by. The Samaritans and the Jews did not like each other. But the Samaritan man still stopped to help the hurt Jewish man.

The Samaritan washed the man's sores and put the man on
his donkey. Then the Samaritan took the hurt man to an
inn where the man could rest and get better. In the morning
when the Samaritan went on his way, he gave the owner of
the inn some money.

"Take care of this hurt man until I come back," the
Samaritan told the owner.

After Jesus told this story, He asked, "Who was a kind neighbor?"

"The one who helped the man," said a listener.

Then Jesus said, "I want you to be a kind neighbor to everyone you meet too!"

Memory Verse
Love your neighbor as yourself.

Luke 10:27b

A Lesson for Martha

Bible story from Luke 10:38-42.

Two sisters named Mary and Martha were good friends of Jesus. Sometimes Jesus came to visit their home. They gladly washed His dusty feet and cooked Him food to eat.

One time when Jesus came to visit, Mary sat and listened to Him teach for a long time. Martha was fixing dinner. She became angry that Mary was not helping her. Martha said to Jesus, "Lord, please tell Mary to come and help me."

"Martha," said Jesus, "don't be upset. Mary has chosen to learn from Me. That is the most important thing she can do with her time."

Jesus was glad Martha cooked for Him. But Mary's choice was even better. Mary chose to learn from Jesus. That pleased Jesus most of all.

Memory Verse
Fix these words of mine in your hearts and minds.

Deuteronomy 11:18a

Selfish People

Bible story from Luke 14:7-11.

A man asked Jesus to come to his house for dinner. People at the dinner party rushed to sit in the best seats. Jesus did not like for the people to be selfish with each other. He talked to the people.

"Do not be selfish," He said. "When a host asks you to come to a dinner party, do not grab the best seat. You should be humble and let other people have the best places.

"If you grab the best for yourself, someone may take it away from you. But if you let others go first, they will treat you as a special friend."

Memory Verse
Do not be proud.

Romans 12:16a

A Sorry Son Goes Home

Bible story from Luke 15:1, 2, 11-24.

Jesus told this story to show how God forgives people who are sorry for their sins.

Once there was a father with two sons. The younger son wanted to leave home. He asked his father for his share of the family's money. Then he packed his clothes and left home. The boy's father was sad to see him go. He knew his son was not wise. And he was afraid his son would get into trouble.

The young man walked and walked. He came to a place where no one knew him. He spent his money on all kinds of things that weren't good for him. Soon his money was all gone.

The young man went to work for a farmer. He fed the farmer's pigs. Sometimes the young man was so hungry, he wanted to eat the pigs' food. The young man was sorry he had left his father. He was sorry he had done bad things.

My father's servants have good food to eat, he thought. *I will go home to my father and tell him I'm sorry for things I've done. Maybe he will let me be one of his servants.*

So the young man left his job with the pigs. He walked and walked and walked. Then finally he saw his house in the distance. Someone was standing in front of it. It was his father. When his father saw him coming, his father ran to meet him.

The boy was thrilled to see his father, and his father was thrilled to see him.

The son said, "Father, I have done wrong. I am not good enough to be your son. May I be one of your servants?"

"No, you are my son. I forgive you." Then the father said to his servants, "Bring some good clothes and shoes for my son. And prepare lots of food. Let's have a party. My son is sorry for what he has done, and now he has come home!"

Memory Verse
You are forgiving and good, O Lord.

Psalm 86:5a

The Forgiven Man

Bible story from Luke 18:9-14.

One day Jesus told this story:

Two men prayed in the temple. One man was a proud Pharisee. The other man was a tax collector.

The Pharisee prayed out loud, "God, I am not like other people. I do only good things. I do not need to say I'm sorry."

The tax collector prayed too. He bowed his head and said, "God, please forgive me. I am sorry for doing wrong things."

The Pharisee really had done wrong things too, but he would not admit it. He was not sorry. The Pharisee did not please God, but the tax collector did. God forgives people who tell Him about the things they do wrong and then ask to be forgiven because they are sorry.

Memory Verse
If we confess our sins, he . . . will forgive us our sins.

I John 1:9a

Zaccheus Is Sorry

Bible story from Luke 19:1-10.

Zaccheus was a tax collector, but he wasn't honest. He made people pay too much tax money. Then he kept some of the money for himself. This made Zaccheus rich, but he did not have many friends.

Zaccheus heard Jesus was coming to town. Everyone was talking about the great stories Jesus told and the wonderful things He did for people. So Zaccheus wanted to see Jesus too.

When someone cried, "Jesus is coming!" a great crowd of people went out to meet Him. Everyone in town wanted to see Jesus. Zacchaeus was very short. He could not see over all the people. So Zacchaeus climbed up a tree beside the road and waited.

Soon Jesus came walking by the tree. Jesus stopped and looked up. He saw Zacchaeus and said to him, "Come down from that tree! I am coming to your house for a visit today!"

Zacchaeus climbed down right away. He led Jesus to his house. The other people were surprised. "Jesus is going to visit the home of a bad man," they said.

But Zacchaeus was sorry he had been bad. He let Jesus know how sorry he was. "I will give half of everything I have to poor people," said Zacchaeus. "And I have taken too much tax money from some people. So I will pay them back four times as much."

Jesus was happy to hear what Zacchaeus had to say. Jesus knew Zacchaeus was really sorry for all the things he had done wrong. He said to Zacchaeus, "I came to help people like you."

Memory Verse
If we confess our sins, he is faithful and just and will forgive us our sins.

I John 1:9a

Jesus Is Friendly

Bible story from John 4:3-42.

Jesus sat down by a well in Samaria. A woman came to get water. She did not talk to Jesus because He was Jewish. Most Jews didn't like the Samaritans.

Jesus asked, "May I have a drink?"

"Why do You ask me?" the woman said.

Jesus said, "I can help you." Jesus told her many things about her life. He also told her about God.

Jesus said, "I am the Savior God promised to send."

The woman ran to get her neighbors. "Come, see a man who told me everything I have ever done. He must be the Savior."

The people came to talk with Jesus. They believed that Jesus was the Savior.

Memory Verse
For we cannot help speaking about what we have seen and heard.
Acts 4:20

Jesus, the King and Savior

Bible story from
Luke 19:29-40; 22:39-42.

Jesus and His helpers were going to Jerusalem. Jesus told two of His helpers to go into a small town near the city.

"You will find a donkey tied up there. Bring it to Me," said Jesus. "Someone may ask you why you are taking the donkey. Tell him that the Lord needs it."

The helpers found the donkey. They said that the Lord needed it. Then they took it to Jesus.

Some helpers put their coats on the donkey's back. Jesus rode the donkey to Jerusalem.

As Jesus went along, people laid their coats and palm branches on the dirt road in front of Him. They did this to show Jesus that they wanted Him to be their new king.

Many people began to shout, "Hosanna! Jesus is our king! He comes in the name of God!" The people waved palm branches as He passed by them.

Some men in the crowd said to Jesus, "Make the people stop shouting and singing."

"No," said Jesus. "Let them shout and sing their songs of praise."

A few nights later Jesus went to a garden where he liked to go to pray. His helpers went with Him, but they soon fell asleep. So Jesus prayed all alone.

Jesus said to God, "Father, I know You want Me to die to save people from their sins. It will be a very hard thing. But I'll do

what You want Me to do. I will be the Savior."

Very soon after that, Jesus did die. The Savior died and came alive again so that we can be in God's family.

Memory Verse
How good it is to sing praises to our God.

Psalms 147:1a

Nicodemus Asks About God's Family

Bible story from John 3:1-21.

Nicodemus was a man who knew a lot about God, but he wanted to know more. One night Nicodemus went to see Jesus. Nicodemus said to Jesus, "Teacher, You make sick people well. You make blind people see. I know You are from God."

Then Jesus said to Nicodemus, "If you want to be in God's family, you must become a new kind of person."

"God sent His Son into the world as a person," said Jesus.

"God's Son will die. He will die for all the bad things that people have done. Everyone who believes in God's Son will live forever in God's family."

Jesus is God's Son. Jesus was talking about Himself! Jesus wanted Nicodemus to be in God's family. Jesus wants everyone to be in God's family. Jesus came to help us all be in God's family forever.

Memory Verse
For God so loved the world that he gave his one and only Son, that whoever believes in him shall not perish but have eternal life.

John 3:16

Mary Worships Jesus

Bible story from John 12:1-8.

Mary and Martha and Lazarus believed that Jesus was the Son of God. He had helped their family many times. They wanted to worship Him in their home.

"Let's give a party for Him," said Martha. "I will cook the food and serve it."

"Good idea," said Lazarus. "Let's thank Jesus for all He's done for us."

"I know a good way to worship Jesus," said Mary. She got some special perfume. It cost a lot of money. At the dinner party Mary knelt by Jesus. She poured the perfume on His feet and dried them with her hair.

The other guests saw how Mary and her family loved Jesus. But best of all, Jesus saw how much they cared. He would always be their best friend.

Memory Verse
Worship the Lord your God and serve him only.

Luke 4:8b

Jesus' Promise

Bible story from John 13:31— 14:14.

The disciples were eating with Jesus. It was their last supper together. "I am going away," Jesus said. "While I am gone, you must love each other as I have loved you."

"Where are You going?" asked Peter.

Jesus said, "To My Father's house. I am going there to prepare a place for you. Someday I will come back and take you to live with Me forever."

The disciples did not understand. "How will we find our way there?"

Jesus said, "You know Me. I am the only way to God."

The disciples felt sad. But Jesus' promise made them feel better! Someday everyone who loves Jesus will go to live with Him forever.

Memory Verse
Jesus answered, "I am the way and the truth and the life."

John 14:6a

Jesus Says Good-bye

Bible story from John 15:9-22; 16:28-33; 17.

Jesus and His disciples were walking. It was late at night. Jesus said, "I am going away soon. When I am gone, remember to love each other. Do all that I have told you."

Jesus said, "You are My friends, and that will get you into trouble. Some people will hate you just as they have hated Me. You must trust Me to still help you when I go to be with My Father."

Jesus prayed for His disciples. "Father, My time on earth is over. Help My disciples and keep them safe. They will tell others about You. Then others will believe that You sent Me. Someday all who believe will be with Me in heaven."

Memory Verse
Go into all the world and preach the good news.

Mark 16:15b

Jesus Died for Us

Bible story from Mark 15:1-39; I Corinthians 15:3.

Jesus, the only Son of God, came to tell others about His Father. But not everyone wanted to hear what He had to say. Some people even hated Jesus. They had Him arrested and brought before Pilate, the governor. "Are You a king?" Pilate asked Jesus.

Jesus said, "Yes, what you say is true."

This made Jesus' enemies very angry. They told lies and said bad things about Him, but Jesus was quiet.

Pilate knew Jesus had done nothing wrong. Pilate said to the people, "This is a special holiday. I can let one prisoner out of jail. Shall I let Jesus go? Or shall I let Barabbas go?" Barabbas was a killer.

"Let Barabbas go! Kill Jesus!" the people yelled.

"What has Jesus done?" asked Pilate.

The people just yelled louder, "Kill Jesus! Put Him on a cross!"

Pilate wasn't happy about what the people wanted, but he had his soldiers take Jesus away. They nailed Jesus to a wooden cross. The people stood around and watched and laughed. "Come down if You are so great," the people yelled.

Jesus could have come down. He could have called an angel army to help, but He stayed on the cross until He died. That was what God, His Father, had asked Him to do.

God asked Jesus to die to take the punishment for everyone's sins. Because Jesus died on the cross, God promises to forgive people's sins and let them be in His special family.

When Jesus died on the cross, a soldier said, "Jesus really was the Son of God!"

Memory Verse
Christ died for our sins.

I Corinthians 15:3b

Mary Shares Good News

Bible story from Luke 23:33; John 20:1-18.

Mary was very sad. Jesus had died on a cross. Now it was early Sunday morning. Mary and some other women were going to Jesus' tomb.

When they got there, the big stone in front of the tomb had been rolled away!

The tomb was open. Jesus' body was not there!

Mary ran to tell Peter and John. "Jesus' body is gone!" she
cried. "He is not in the tomb."

Peter and John ran to the tomb. John got there first. But he
didn't go inside until Peter got there. Peter and John saw that
Jesus was gone. But they didn't know where He was.
So they went away from the tomb.

Mary went to the tomb again. She began to cry.
She looked inside the tomb and saw two angels.

"Why are you crying?" the angels asked. "They have taken Jesus," Mary said. "I don't know where they have put Him."

Then Mary turned and saw someone. He was standing near the tomb. She thought it was the gardener. He said, "Why are you crying? Who is it you are looking for?"

Mary said, "Sir, if you took Jesus away, please tell me where you put Him."

"Mary," the man said.

Mary saw that it was Jesus. Jesus was alive! "Teacher!" Mary said.

Mary was not sad anymore. She went to Jesus' friends. What good news she had to tell them! "I have seen Jesus," said Mary. "Jesus is alive!"

Memory Verse
He is not here; he has risen, just as he said.

Matthew 28:6a

Not Alone

Bible story from Luke 24:36-43; John 20:19-29.

Jesus' helpers met together in secret after Jesus died. They were afraid the soldiers would come and get them, too. Suddenly, Jesus was in the room with them. "Peace be with you!" He said.

The helpers saw the nail marks in Jesus' hands and feet. Could it be Jesus? Was He really there?

Jesus said, "Why do you doubt?" Then He ate a piece of the fish to show them He was alive. When they saw Him eat the food, they knew it was true.

Thomas, one of Jesus' helpers, did not see Jesus. Thomas doubted Jesus was alive. But the next time Jesus came, Thomas was there. Jesus said, "See the nail marks. Do not doubt; just believe."

Thomas said, "Oh, Jesus, it IS You!"

Jesus said, "You believe I am alive because you see Me. How happy the people will be who believe without seeing Me!"

Memory Verse
And surely I am with you always, to the very end of the age.

Matthew 28:20b

Peter's Special Job

Bible story from John 21:1-17.

Some of Jesus' disciples went fishing one night. But they caught no fish in their nets. As they rowed their boat back to shore, they saw a man standing on the beach. He shouted to them, "Throw out your net again."

When they did, fish filled the net. John said, "That man is Jesus!" Peter jumped out and splashed his way to the shore as fast as he could go.

Later Jesus asked Peter, "Do you love Me?"

"Yes, Lord," answered Peter. "You know I do."

"Then take care of My sheep," Jesus said.

Jesus' sheep are all the people who love Him. Peter's special job was to help people and tell them about Jesus. Jesus wants His followers to listen and learn from those who teach us about Jesus.

Memory Verse
Respect those who work hard among you, who are over you in the Lord.

I Thessalonians 5:12b

Jesus Goes to Heaven

Bible story from Luke 24:50-53; Acts 1:8-14.

Jesus died and came alive again. Many people saw Jesus after He came alive. He spent time with His helpers teaching them the things they needed to know before He went away.

One day Jesus took His helpers for a walk up a big hill.

When they came to the top, Jesus stopped and said, "Wait for God's Holy Spirit. He will help you be My witnesses. Go and tell other people about Me. Tell people here. Tell people in other lands. Tell people all over the world."

As the helpers stood there listening to Jesus, Jesus began to rise up off the ground! Soon He was so high in the sky that a cloud covered Him. Jesus' helpers didn't know what to think. They just stood there looking up into the sky.

Suddenly two angels dressed all in white were beside them. "Why are you looking up into the sky?" the angels asked. "Jesus has gone up to heaven. You saw Him go. He will come back someday the same way."

Then Jesus' friends went back to the city. They prayed together and waited for the Special Helper Jesus promised to send them.

"Thank You, God, for sending Jesus," the friends prayed. "Thank You for making Jesus live again. Help us do what You want. We will work for You until Jesus comes back again."

Memory Verse
I will come back and take you to be with me.

John 14:3b

Saul's New Job

Bible story from Acts 9:1-22.

Saul did not believe in Jesus, and he hated people who did. One day he set out for the town of Damascus to find some of Jesus' friends. It was Saul's job to put them in jail. As Saul was walking down the road, a bright light suddenly shone down from heaven. Saul fell to the ground as he heard a voice say, "Saul, why do you hurt Me?"

"Who are You, Lord?" asked Saul.

The answer came back, "I am Jesus."

When Saul got up, he could not see. His friends helped him walk to Damascus. There he met a man named Ananias. Jesus had talked to Ananias in a vision and told him to put his hands on Saul's eyes. When he did, Saul could see again.

Saul changed his name to Paul. Now he believed Jesus was God's Son. So God gave Paul a new job. He asked him to tell people about His Savior, Jesus.

Memory Verse
There are different kinds of service, but the same Lord.

I Corinthians 12:5

Paul Gets Busy

Bible story from Matthew 28:18-20; Acts 9:15; 13:1-5.

Before Jesus went back to heaven, He told His disciples, "Tell people from all countries about Me. Baptize them and teach them to obey Me."

Paul was one of the men God chose to go from city to city teaching people about Jesus.

A man named Barnabas asked Paul to come to his church in Antioch. Then he and Paul taught the people of Antioch how to obey Jesus.

One day as the people of Antioch were worshiping,
God's Holy Spirit spoke to them: "I have a job for
Paul and Barnabas. They are to be My missionaries. Help
them do the work I have for them."

The church prayed for Paul and Barnabas. Then the two men
started on a trip. They went from place to place teaching
people about Jesus. They were missionaries for Jesus.

Memory Verse
Therefore go and make disciples of all nations.

Matthew 28:19a

Dorcas Helps Others

Bible story from Acts 9:36-42.

Dorcas lived in the city of Joppa. She had many friends. She loved Jesus and wanted to please Him. So she used her time and money to help others.

Dorcas knew how to sew. She made beautiful clothes. Whenever she saw a poor child or woman, she made this person something new to wear.

Stitch after stitch she sewed with love. It made her happy to see her poor friends wearing warm, clean clothes that she had made.

"I like to look nice and I know they do too," she said to herself. "And I know that this is what God wants me to do. He has given me everything I need. So I want to share what I have with others."

One day Dorcas felt sick. Her friends were worried. She always took care of them. Now what could they do for her? They tried everything they could think of to help her, but nothing worked. Dorcas died and her friends all cried.

Then one friend said, "I heard that one of Jesus' disciples named Peter is nearby in the town of Lydda. Perhaps he can help Dorcas. God has given him great power to heal the sick." So Dorcas's friends sent two men to Lydda to get Peter.

Peter agreed to go with the men to Joppa to see Dorcas. When he arrived at her home, Dorcas's friends showed him all of the clothes Dorcas had made for them. Peter could tell how much Dorcas loved Jesus by the kind things she did for other people.

Peter went to Dorcas's room to pray for her. He knelt beside her bed and talked to God. Then he looked at Dorcas and said, "Dorcas, get up!"

Dorcas opened her eyes and sat up. Then Peter took her hand and led her downstairs to her friends. Everyone was very happy. And many people in Joppa believed in Jesus because of Peter and Dorcas.

Memory Verse
And let us consider how we may spur one another on toward love and good deeds.

Hebrews 10:24

Christians Give an Offering

Bible story from Acts 11:22-30.

Paul and Barnabas went to a church in a town called Antioch. There they taught the people about Jesus from God's Word.

One day a message came from the church in Jerusalem. It said, "A famine is coming. Soon it will be hard to grow food. The people in the church of Jerusalem will not have enough food."

The Christians in Antioch said, "We want to help the church in Jerusalem. They helped us by sending Paul and Barnabas to

teach us about Jesus. We will help them have food to eat."

So the people in Antioch took an offering. They sent the money to the church in Jerusalem.

The people in the Jerusalem church were very happy to get the money. They said to Paul and Barnabas, "We are glad for the Christians at Antioch! We are thankful for their help."

Memory Verse
God loves a cheerful giver.

II Corinthians 9:7b

Peter Is Set Free

Bible story from Acts 12:1-19.

After Jesus went to heaven, His disciples went from place to place telling people about Jesus. King Herod knew that many people in his kingdom did not like Jesus' disciples. So King Herod had the disciple James arrested and put to death. This made Jesus' enemies very happy. So King Herod had Peter arrested too.

Peter was put in jail and chained between two soldiers. One night God sent an angel to rescue Peter. A bright light shown in the jail cell and Peter's chains fell off. The two guards with Peter didn't hear or see a thing. They just kept on sleeping.

"Get up and get dressed," the angel said. "Then follow me." Peter did as the angel said. It was almost like a dream. They walked past guards who didn't see them. Locked gates opened without a key.

Soon Peter found himself standing on the street all alone. "It was not a dream. I'm free!" Peter said to himself. So he hurried to the home of a friend where many people had gathered to pray for Peter.

Bang, bang, bang! Peter pounded on the door. "Who could that be?" the people inside asked each other. "It's late. Could it be soldiers coming to arrest us, too?"

Rhoda, a servant girl, went to the door and asked, "Who is it?"

"It's me, Peter," she heard the man answer. Rhoda was so excited, she ran back to tell the others.

"Are you sure it's Peter?" everyone asked Rhoda.

"Yes, it really is him. I know his voice," she said. Then she ran back and opened the door. Everyone was so happy to see Peter and hear about his great escape.

"How good it is to know that nothing is too hard for God," they all said.

Memory Verse
Nothing is too hard for you.

Jeremiah 32:17b

A Miracle and a Mistake

Bible story from Acts 14:6-18.

Paul and Barnabas were missionaries. They went to many places telling people the good news about Jesus. Many people began to believe in Him.

One day as Paul began to preach about Jesus, he saw a man who was lame listening to him. Paul could tell that the man believed Jesus could make him well. "Stand up on your feet!" said Paul.

The man stood up. He could walk!

The other people in the city saw this. They did not understand that it was Jesus' power that made the lame man well. They thought that Paul and Barnabas made the man well all by themselves.

The people pointed to Paul and Barnabas. "These men are gods!" they said. The people wanted to worship Paul and Barnabas.

"Stop!" shouted Paul and Barnabas. "We are not gods. We are just people like you."

"We came to tell you the good news that there is a real, living God. We want you to forget false gods. The real, living God made everything. He sends rain from heaven and helps you have the food you need."

Paul and Barnabas talked and talked, but it was hard for the people to understand. They could see Paul and Barnabas, but they could not see God.

Soon Paul and Barnabas had to leave that city. They had more missionary work to do. They had to keep preaching about Jesus. They knew Jesus would give them power to do their work for Him.

Memory Verse
If anyone serves, he should do it with the strength God provides.
I Peter 4:11a

Learning to Be a Good Worker

Bible story from Acts 12:25—13:13, 15:36-41;
Colossians 4:10; II Timothy 4:11

John Mark wanted to be a missionary like Paul and Barnabas. He offered to be their helper. So, the three men traveled to a faraway land to tell people about Jesus. The trip was not easy, and John Mark decided to quit and go home.

The next time Paul and Barnabas planned a trip, Barnabas asked if John Mark could come too. Paul said, "No, he isn't a good worker. He quits."

"Jesus can help him learn to be a good worker," said Barnabas. But Paul still said no. This made Barnabas angry. He wanted to give John Mark another chance.

So Paul traveled with his friend, Silas, and Barnabas traveled with John Mark. This time John Mark did not quit. And he did learn to be a good worker. Even Paul said so!

Memory Verse
Always give yourselves fully to the work of the Lord.
I Corinthians 15:58b

A Busy Time for Paul and Silas

Bible story from Acts 16:12-40.

Paul knew that there were still many people who had never heard about Jesus. So Paul went on another missionary trip. This time a man named Silas went with Paul to help him.

One day Paul and Silas came to a place where some women were praying. One of the women was named Lydia. Lydia and the other women knew about God. But they did not know about God's Son. So Paul told them all about Jesus.

Lydia believed what Paul said about Jesus. She and her family were baptized. Paul and Silas stayed at her house.

One day Paul and Silas met a slave girl. This girl made money for her owners by telling people what was going to happen in the future.

Paul knew that it was wrong for the girl to do this. So Paul prayed for her, and Jesus helped her stop. This made the girl's owners very angry. They had Paul and Silas put in jail.

Paul and Silas kept trusting Jesus even though they were in jail. They prayed and sang songs to God.

At midnight there was a great earthquake. It shook the jail, and the doors flew open. The chains fell off of everyone. The jailer was sure that his prisoners had all escaped. So he decided it would be better to die rather than be punished for losing them.

Paul and Silas called out, "Don't hurt yourself. Everyone is still here."

The jailer was so happy to hear their voices. He asked Paul and Silas, "What can I do to be saved?"

Paul and Silas answered, "If you believe in the Lord Jesus, you will be saved."

The jailer did believe and invited them to tell his family about Jesus. Then his whole family believed in Jesus.

They were all in God's family now, so Paul and Silas baptized them.

The next day Paul and Silas got out of jail. They had more missionary work to do. Soon they left to help people in other places know about Jesus and believe in Him.

Memory Verse
Go into all the world and preach the good news to all creation.

Mark 16:15b

Paul Helps a Church

Bible story from Acts 18:1-11.

Paul went to the city of Corinth. Aquila and his wife, Priscilla, made tents in this city. Paul stayed and worked with them.

Every week Paul went out to tell people about Jesus. Paul wanted people to believe in Jesus and become part of God's church. Soon Paul began spending all of his time teaching people about Jesus.

Some people did not like what Paul had to say, but many people believed in Jesus.

Jesus talked to Paul in a vision. Jesus said, "Keep on teaching the people about Me. I will be with you."

So Paul kept on preaching and the church kept on growing. Paul helped them grow to be like Jesus.

Memory Verse
Serve the Lord with all your heart.

I Samuel 12:20b

Apollos Listens and Learns

Bible story from Acts 18:24-28.

Paul's good friends, Priscilla and Aquila, moved to the city of Ephesus. They were leather workers like Paul. They made tents and purses and other useful things. They were also followers of Jesus, and they were very good teachers.

One day a man from Egypt came to town. He was a Jew from the city of Alexandria. Alexandria was known for its great school and library. The man's name was Apollos.

Apollos spoke at the synagogue in Ephesus. Priscilla and Aquila thought he was a very fine speaker. Apollos believed in Jesus, but there were many things he didn't know about Him.

Priscilla and Aquila invited Apollos to their home. Then they taught him more about Jesus. Apollos was glad they helped him. He used the things he learned to become a good teacher like Aquila and Priscilla.

Memory Verse
Pay attention and listen to the sayings of the wise.

Proverbs 22:17a

Jesus Takes Care of Paul

Bible story from Acts 27.

Paul was a missionary for Jesus. He talked about Jesus wherever he went. But some people did not like that. And they had Paul put in prison.

One day Paul and some other prisoners got on a big sailing ship. A centurion and his soldiers went along to guard the prisoners. They were sailing to a city called Rome.

It was almost winter when the ship left. The sea was rough and the wind was cold. Paul knew it wasn't safe to be sailing.

"The weather is bad," Paul said. "We should not keep on sailing. Our ship might be wrecked in a storm, and everyone on the ship might be hurt."

But no one would listen to Paul. "Keep on sailing," said the centurion.

Soon a terrible storm began. The wind made the ship rock back and forth. Waves crashed across the deck. The sky was as dark as night, and it rained and rained for several days and nights.

All the people on the ship were afraid. "We will die in this storm," they cried.

But Paul said to the people, "Be brave! An angel of God visited me last night. He promised that we will all live, but our ship will be wrecked."

Soon the ship was close to land. The centurion told everyone what to do. He said, "If you can swim, swim to the shore. If you can't swim, hold onto boards. Then you can float to shore."

The people on the ship did as he said. And all of them were kept safe. Paul was kept safe too. Jesus took good care of Paul.

Memory Verse
My grace is sufficient for you, for my power is made perfect in weakness.

II Corinthians 12:9a

Timothy Learns God's Word

Bible story from
II Timothy 1:1-5; 3:14-17.

Timothy was a little boy when he first learned about God. His mother and his grandmother taught little Timothy from God's Word, the Scriptures.

"Pay attention, Timothy," said his mother. "God will teach you in the Scriptures what is right and what is wrong."

"Pay attention, Timothy," said his grandmother. "The Scriptures tell us what God is like. He loves us and wants us to obey Him."

Timothy paid attention when his mother and grandmother told him stories from Scripture. As Timothy grew older he learned to read the Scriptures too. But most important, Timothy learned to love God. And because he loved God, Timothy wanted to do the things that pleased God.

Timothy learned from the Scriptures that God didn't want him to steal and lie. Timothy tried not to do these things. Timothy also learned from the Scriptures that God wanted him to help people forgive and share the things God gave him. Timothy tried to do these things.

427

One day, when Timothy was a young man, Paul came to Timothy's town. Paul said, "Jesus is God's Son. The Scriptures said that God would send Jesus. God wants you to believe in Jesus."

Timothy's mother said, "I will believe in Jesus."

Timothy said, "I will believe in Jesus."

Some time later, Paul came back and talked to Timothy. "Timothy, you know the Scriptures well. You would be a good

helper for me. We will teach people what the Scriptures say about Jesus. We will teach people to love and obey Jesus."

Timothy was glad he had paid attention when his family taught him God's Word. All that he learned helped him be a good worker for God.

Memory Verse
I have set my heart on your laws.

Psalm 119:30b

Paul's Friends Help Him
Bible story from Philippians 4:10-23.

Paul was a missionary for Jesus. Some people wanted to stop Paul from preaching. So they had him arrested.

Many of Paul's friends lived far away. But they wanted to help Paul. They knew he needed to have money so he could buy food and clothes. So they collected money to give to Paul. A man traveled a long way to bring the money to him. Paul was pleased by this gift of love.

He wrote his friends a letter. "Dear friends, your gift made me happy! It is not that I need much money to live on. I can be happy if I have nothing, because God gives me the strength and courage I need.

"I know your gift of love to me made God happy too. He will remember the good things you do. And He will give you all that you need."

Memory Verse
It is more blessed to give than to receive.

Acts 20:35b

Paul Trusts Jesus

Bible story from Acts 21:10-14, 27-36; 23:11-35.

Paul was going to Jerusalem. Paul's friends warned him not to go. "Some people in that city will try to stop you from telling others about Jesus," they said. But Paul trusted God to help him, and so he went.

God helped Paul be brave when Paul got to Jerusalem. Some men told lies about Paul and a crowd of people tried to hurt him. Then soldiers came and arrested Paul and put him in jail.

The men who didn't like Paul got together to talk. They made

a secret plan to kill him. But Paul's nephew was nearby. He heard their plan and told Paul and the soldiers guarding Paul all about it.

The soldiers sneaked Paul out of town at night so his enemies could not kill him.

God didn't let Paul's enemies harm him. Paul trusted God. And God helped him be brave.

Memory Verse
But let us encourage one another.

Hebrews 10:25b

The Sorry Servant

Bible story from Philemon 1-25.

Onesimus did not like being a servant. He worked for a man named Philemon. One day Onesimus did something wrong, and he ran away from Philemon.

Onesimus headed for the big city of Rome. A big city was a good place to hide. But Paul was in Rome, and Paul was a friend of Philemon's. Somehow Paul and Onesimus met. Paul told Onesimus about Jesus. Onesimus believed what Paul said and decided to become part of the church.

Now Onesimus was sorry for the wrong things he had done and for running away from Philemon.

Paul sent a letter to his friend Philemon. The letter said, "Dear Philemon, You are part of God's church because you believe in Jesus. Onesimus is part of the church too. I am sending him back to you. You should show love to him because it is what Jesus wants you to do."

Memory Verse
Dear friends, let us love one another, for love comes from God.

I John 4:7a

John Writes About God's Family

Bible story from I John 3; Revelation 21—22.

God told John to write a letter. John wrote, "God loves us very much. He showed us this by sending us Jesus. Now God calls us His children because we believe in His Son, Jesus. We are God's family, the church. Because of this, God does not want us to do wrong things. God wants us to love one another and do what is right. We can show our love for God by helping others in God's family."

God also showed John what would happen in the future. God showed John what heaven will be like. John wrote down the things God showed him: "God's family will live in heaven. We will stay there with Jesus forever. We can look forward to this because God has promised it and God's words are true."

Memory Verse
How good and pleasant it is when brothers live together in unity!
Psalm 133:1

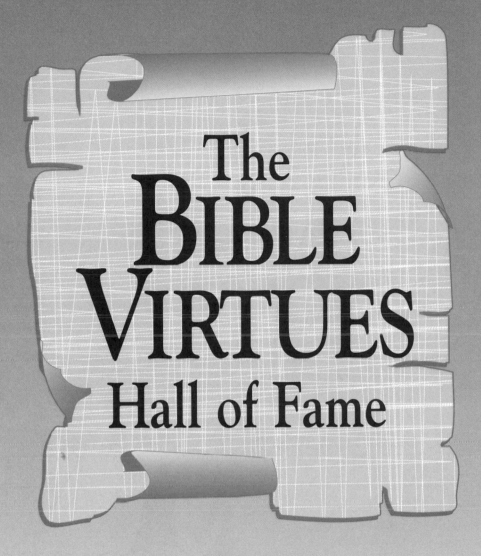

The
BIBLE
VIRTUES
Hall of Fame

The Bible Virtues Hall of Fame

BEING HOLY–Paul

In the book of Romans, Paul tells Christians that God wants us to be holy. To be holy means we should be like God. We should be honest, loving, and we should want to do what is right at all times. When your friends want you to do something wrong, are you willing to tell them no? Are you willing to be holy?

PRAISE–Deborah

The Bible says we should praise God. When we praise God, we tell Him how wonderful He is. Deborah was a wise woman who praised God. When God gave the Israelites victory over their enemies, Deborah led them in a song of praise. We can read the words of her song in Judges 5. What has God done for you? How can you praise Him?

FAITH–Abraham

The Bible says that we should have faith in God. Faith is believing that God will do the things He has promised. Abraham was a man of faith. He obeyed God even when he didn't understand why God asked him to do something. When God promised to give Abraham a son, he believed God even though Abraham and his wife Sarah were very old. Abraham showed his faith in God many other times, too. Do you trust God to keep His promises to you?

COURAGE–Esther

There are many stories in the Bible about courage. Courage is a willingness to do what needs to be done when faced with danger. Queen Esther risked losing her own life to save her people. Even though she was afraid, she didn't let her fears stop her from going to see the king. Do you have enough courage to do what's right when you are faced with a big problem?

WISDOM–King Solomon

The Bible says that King Solomon was the wisest man who ever lived. Being wise is different from being smart. Wisdom is a gift from God. People who are wise put what they know to good use by choosing to follow and obey God. How are you putting the things you are learning to good use? Have you asked God to give you wisdom?

OBEDIENCE–Jonah

There are many stories in the Bible about obedience. Obedience is doing what you are told to do. God wants His people to obey Him. Jonah learned this lesson the hard way. He tried to run away from God because he didn't want to obey. Jonah spent three days in the belly of a big fish thinking about the trouble he'd caused himself by disobeying God. Can you think of a time you got in trouble for not obeying? Why is obeying God, your parents, and your teachers the best idea?

RESPONSIBILITY–
Nehemiah

The Bible says that we should be responsible people. That means that we can be trusted to do what we promise. Responsible people are willing to do their fair share of the work. Nehemiah was a responsible person. He helped his people rebuild the city walls of Jerusalem, and he didn't quit until the job was done. Are you responsible in helping with chores around your home? Do you finish the jobs you start?

LOYALTY–Ruth

There are many examples of loyal people in the Bible. One of the most famous is Ruth. To be loyal means that you protect and care for someone—no matter what. They can depend on you. Ruth was very loyal to her mother-in-law, Naomi. After Naomi's husband and sons died, Ruth took care of her. Who can you depend on? Who is loyal to you? To whom are you loyal? Are you loyal to God? When someone you know uses God's name in the wrong way, do you stick up for God and tell this person to stop doing it?

JOYFULNESS–Paul and Silas

The Bible says that God wants His people to be joyful. Being joyful is the best kind of good feeling you can have. Joyfulness is better than happiness, because it lasts even when something bad happens. Paul and Silas were beaten and thrown in jail for telling people about Jesus, but they still felt joyful. They knew that God was with them and that He loved them and would take care of them. When bad things happen to you, are you still joyful because you know God cares about you and wants to help?

LOVE–Mary and Joseph

There is no better place in the world to learn about real love than in the Bible. That's because no one knows more about

love than God, and the Bible is His Word. Love is more than just liking someone a lot, love is an action. When we love someone it shows in the things we say and do. God says He loves us the way a father and mother love their children. Mary and Joseph showed this special love for Jesus by teaching Him God's Word and helping him grow up into a fine young man. How do your parents show that they love you? How do you show that you love them? How does God show His love for us?

THANKFULNESS–
Noah

The Bible says that we should be thankful for all that God has done for us. Thankfulness is a feeling of appreciation. When someone does something nice for us, we should say thank you to let the person know that we like or appreciate what they have done. When God saved Noah and his family from the flood, Noah remembered to thank God. God was glad

and promised never to flood the earth again. God is pleased when we thank Him. Have you thanked God for all He's done for you?

HELPFULNESS–
Moses

The Bible tells us that God wants His followers to be like a great big family. He wants us to help each other. Moses helped the Israelites leave Egypt and travel to the promised land. When the job of taking care of God's people got too hard for Moses to handle alone, God helped Moses choose good helpers. What do you need help with? Who can help you? How are you helping others?

Faith Parenting
Guide

The Children's Discovery Bible

AGE: 3-6 Read to Me; 5-8 Read It Myself

LIFE ISSUE: My child is learning that Bible characters are good examples of many values.

VALUE: Being Holy, Praise, Faith, Courage, Wisdom, Obedience, Responsibility, Loyalty, Joyfulness, Love, Thankfulness, Helpfulness, and More!

Parent Interactivity: Read a chapter at a time to your child and then interact with him or her by using one or more of the following ideas. Try to choose ideas that teach your child in his or her primary learning style.

Visual Learning Style: (I learn with my eyes.) The "Bible Virtues Hall of Fame" (pages 440-445) is a good bouncing off point for visual-oriented activities. Here's one idea: You can create your own "Biblical Values *Wall* of Fame." Tape a large piece of newsprint to your child's wall. Each time you read a chapter or a series of chapters in *The Children's Discovery Bible* about a particular Bible character, help your child draw a picture of the character. Discuss how the Bible character modeled a particular value (see pages 440-445 for examples). Finally, write the name of that value under the picture. For additional reinforcement, look for examples of people modeling biblical values in newspaper and magazine stories; cut these out and paste or tape them to your mural. On special occasions to encourage your child, paste photographs or draw pictures of him or her modeling a particular biblical value. Alternate method: Photocopy and cut out the pictures and paragraphs from page 440-445 and paste or tape these to a large sheet of newsprint.

Auditory Learning Style: (I learn with my ears.) One of the ways auditory learners learn best is through question and answer times. Each time you finish reading a chapter in *The Children's Discovery Bible,* discuss what value was practiced (or, if appropriate, what value was not practiced; for example, in the story of the Tower of Babel, the people did not practice the value of humility). Use different questions each time, but let's say you were discussing the story of Esther and the value of courage. You might discuss questions like: *What is courage? Did Esther do a good job practicing the value of courage? How? How do you think God feels when we practice the value of courage? How do you think other people feel? Is there any place in your life where you need to practice courage? What can you do?* No matter what value you're discussing, never pass up an opportunity to encourage your child by pointing out times that you have seen him or her practice the value you are discussing.

Tactile Learning Style: (I learn by doing things.) One of the ways a tactile learner learns best is through object lessons. Some great sources for finding more object lessons that reinforce biblical values are the Family Night Tool Chest books in the Heritage Builders series. Here are a few examples of ways to use object lessons in the Family Night books to complement what your child is reading in *The Children's Discovery Bible:*

IDEA 1: "Big Boat, Big Job"
Value: Persistence
Adapted from page 83-84 of *Christian Character Qualities* in the Family Night Tool Chest series.
Related story in *The Children's Discovery Bible:* "Noah Obeys God," pages 34-35.
Work on completing a jigsaw puzzle with your child. Be sure to choose a puzzle with a difficulty level appropriate for your child, and one you can complete in a short amount of time. Make this task a little more challenging by not showing your child the finished picture. It's important to help your children get a sense of satisfaction from completing the puzzle. Then discuss the persistence it takes to complete a job that seems too hard to finish at first. Review how Noah completed a big, difficult job by obeying God and building an ark.

IDEA 2: "A-MAZING COURAGE"
Value: Courage
Adapted from page 94 of *Christian Character Qualities* in the Family Night Tool Chest series.
Related story in *The Children's Discovery Bible:* "Esther saves her people," pages 240-245.
Create a simple maze in your living room. Stand on a chair at the end of the maze and ask your child to keep his or her eyes on you at all times while going through the maze. Recruit other family members or friends to stand on the sides of the maze and try to distract your child by yelling, telling jokes, etc. Talk with your children about how others will try to distract us from living our lives focused on God. Discuss how it takes courage to take a stand against the people who distract us and tempt us and to stay focused on God instead. Review how Esther took a stand for God despite being distracted and tempted by others like Haman.

IDEA 3: "GOD CAN DO IT"
Value: Faithfulness
Adapted from page 31-33 of *Christian Character Qualities* in the Family Night Tool Chest series.
Related story in *The Children's Discovery Bible:* "Jesus Uses a Boy's Lunch," pages 310-313.
Ask if your child thinks he or she can lift you off the ground. Let your child try until he or she concludes that the task is impossible. Then bring out a sturdy plank of wood (six or more inches wide and six to eight feet long) and a brick or other object to work as a fulcrum. Stand at one end of the plank and have your child stand on the other end. Adjust the fulcrum (move it closer to the side you are standing on) until your child's weight is enough to lift you off the ground. Discuss how your child can—with God's help—do things that seem impossible. Review how Jesus did what seemed impossible when He fed a large crowd with one boy's lunch.